HORSE TRAINING:
OUTDOOR AND HIGH SCHOOL

By ÉTIENNE BEUDANT
Former Captain, French Cavalry

With a Preface
By M. TH. MONOD
Senior Veterinarian 1st Class
Director of Troop Veterinary Service
Chief of Breeding, French Remount Service in Morocco

And an Introduction
By LT. COL. JOHN A. BARRY,
U. S. Cavalry

© Xenophon Press 2014

Copyright © 1931 Charles Scribner's Sons

Copyright © 2014 by Xenophon Press LLC

Translated by John A. Barry

Edited and Translated by Richard F. Williams

All rights reserved. No part of this work may be reproduced or transmitted in any form or by any means, electronic or mechanical, including photocopying, or by any information storage or retrieval system except by a written permission from the publisher.

Published by Xenophon Press LLC

7518 Bayside Road, Franktown, Virginia 23354-2106, U.S.A.

ISBN-10   0933316461
ISBN-13   9780933316461

Cover design by Naia E. Poyer

e-book ISBN-10: 0933316534
e-book ISBN-13: 9780933316539

CONTENTS

Table of Illustrations	iii
Preface to the Xenophon Press Edition	v
DEDICATION	vii
PREFACE	ix
INTRODUCTION	xi
HORSE TRAINING	1
METHODS	9
HANDS WITHOUT LEGS, LEGS WITHOUT HANDS	24
DEFINITIONS	25
TACT	25
AIDS	25
IMPULSION	26
ACTION	27
POSITION	27
MOVEMENT	27
BALANCE	28
BEHIND THE AIDS	29
TO SEPARATE THE FORCE AND THE MOVEMENT	30
THE STRAIGHT HORSE	30
SUPPORT REIN	31
DIAGONAL EFFECTS	31
THE DESCENT OF THE HAND AND THE LEG	32
LIGHTNESS	33
LIGHTNESS TO THE HANDS	34
HANDS	35
VIBRATION	35
HALF-HALT	35
FLEXIONS OF THE JAW	35
THE MOUTH	37
BITTING	37
ACTION OF THE HANDS	38
GOOD HANDS	39
LIGHTNESS OF THE HAUNCHES	39
PROGRESSION OF DRESSAGE	41
TO MOUNT WITH THE HELP OF AN ASSISTANT	41
TO MOVE THE HORSE FORWARD	41
TO HALT	41
TO REIN-BACK	41
TO TURN	41

TO SIDE STEP	41
PIROUETTES	41
CIRCLES, HALF-CIRCLES, DIAGONAL CHANGE OF HAND	42
OBEDIENCE TO THE SPUR	42
ORDINARY TRAINING	42
ADVANCED TRAINING	42
MARCH ON THE SPUR	43
SUPPORT OF THE SPUR AT THE WALK	43
FROM THE WALK TO THE TROT ON THE SPUR	44
EFFET D'ENSEMBLE ON THE SPUR	44
ACCORD OF THE AIDS	46
THE *RAMENER*	46
THE *RASSEMBLER*	47
DIFFERENCE BETWEEN *EFFET D'ENSEMBLE* AND *RASSEMBLER*	48
WORK AT THE CANTER	48
THE GRAND TROT	53
JUMPING	54
OUT-OF-DOORS [OUTDOOR RIDING]	58
HAUTE ÉCOLE	60
AIRS OF FANTASY	66
RESULTS OF TRAINING	81
CONCLUSIONS	120

ILLUSTRATIONS

The Passage	5
Robersart II Jumping	6
Major-General Guy V. Henry	7
A French Officer	13
Signor Alvisi	19
Point-to-Point at Pau	24
Major Cole	29
International Horse Show at Nice	38
Major Cafaretti	43
Captain McMahon	49
International Horse Show at Nice	52
Captain Lequio	55
Captain Count Borsarelli	56
Left at the Post	57
Captain Bradford, Buckaroo	59
Lieutenant Wofford	63
Lieutenant-Colonel Merchant	64
The *Piaffer*	67
The *Passage*	68
Action!	72
The Trot-to-Rear	73
The Spanish Trot	74
Extended Trot	76
The Gallop-to-Rear	77
The Gallop on Three Legs	78
Mabrouk, The Peacock	79
Buckaroo, Captain Bradford	84
Interallied Horse Show at Coblenz, 1920	86
Bank and Bar	92
Captain Gerhardt	98
Captain Calvi	102
Captain Carr	116
A Triple, Captain Bradford	117
Major Doak	121
Major Chamberlin	122

Xenophon Press Library

Xenophon Press is dedicated to the preservation of classical equestrian literature.
Available at **www.XenophonPress.com.**

30 Years with Master Nuno Oliveira, Michel Henriquet 2011
A Rider's Survival from Tyranny, Charles de Kunffy 2012
Another Horsemanship, Jean-Claude Racinet, 1994
Art of the Lusitano, Yglesias de Oliveira 2012
Baucher and His School, General Decarpentry 2011
Dressage in the French Tradition, Dom Diogo de Bragança 2011
École de Cavalerie Part II, François Robichon de la Guérinière 1992
François Baucher: The Man and His Method, Baucher/Nelson 2013
Gymnastic Exercises for Horses Volume II, Eleanor Russell 2013
H. Dv. 12 Cavalry Manual of Horsemanship, Reinhold 2014
Healing Hands, Dominique Giniaux, DVM 1998
Horse Training: Outdoors and High School by Étienne Beudant 2014
Legacy of Master Nuno Oliveira, Stephanie Millham 2013
Methodical Dressage of the Riding Horse, Faverot de Kerbrech 2010
Racinet Explains Baucher, Jean-Claude Racinet 1997
The Art of Traditional Dressage, Volume I DVD, de Kunffy 2013
Great Horsewomen of the 19th Century in the Circus, Nelson 2001
The Ethics and Passions of Dressage Expanded Ed., de Kunffy 2013
The Gymnasium of the Horse, Gustav Steinbrecht 2011
The Italian Tradition of Equestrian Art, Tomassini 2014
The Maneige Royal, Antoine de Pluvinel 2010
The Portuguese School of Equestrian Art, de Oliveira/da Costa 2012
The Science and Art of Riding with Lightness, Stodulka 2014
The Spanish Riding School & Piaffe and Passage, Decarpentry 2013
Total Horsemanship, Jean-Claude Racinet 1999
Wisdom of Master Nuno Oliveira, Antoine de Coux 2012

Preface to the Xenophon Press Edition

We are pleased to present in this revised English edition of the earlier American edition of 1931. Wherever possible images have been clarified or enlarged. While John Barry provided a starting point for the translation, many sections have been re-translated from the original French edition for the sake of clarity and accuracy. Hence, Beudant's meaning has been established with this edition's text remaining as true to the French meaning as possible. The word "gallop" in this text is referring to the French word and in most cases means "canter," unless the author is writing about cross-country riding or a "full" or "flat out" gallop. Xenophon Press wishes to thank Stephanie Millham for her tireless line-editing of this work.

It is with great appreciation that we extend our thanks to Charles Scribner and Sons for their cooperation in allowing the use of the 1931 material. Our readers have been asking us for this missing link between Faverot de Kerbrech, General L'Hotte and Nuno Oliveira and Rene Bacharach for years.

Xenophon Press is committed to bridging the gaps in chronology of equestrian literature in the English language. Étienne Beudant's unique contribution is difficult to put into words. His philosophy must be read, experienced. It is simple, and profound. Seemingly obvious—in front of us at all times—and yet—illusive to so many. His stories of his many horses are perhaps the most educational. Through these examples, we understand his theory, his practice proved his principles and he even surprised himself many times. Compassion for the horse comes through to us even though Beudant expected and enabled the greatest noble and athletic performance from each.

Richard F. Wiliams
Publisher/Translator
Xenophon Press LLC

To General of Division Juinot-Gambetta:

My dear General: At the beginning of the war you expressly promised to send me to the great battle-front.

Then came my accident and, alas! You could not send me—either to France or to the East, where by the brilliant capture of Uskub, you paved the way to final victory.

Pain, only pain which never quits me, mitigates the bitterness of my inaction. All is over for me—no more the joy of equitation, an art that has so obsessed me as to bring the reproach of devoting overmuch time to it.

Many horsemen have asked me to publish the notes I made on the horses I trained in Morocco. These notes were sent to M. Monod, Director of Veterinary Service and Chief of the Breeding Bureau, as the horses were being trained. This learned veterinarian himself is particularly insistent, and, I would be extremely ungracious to refuse, because all I have done has been to practice the equitation doctrines of General Faverot de Kerbrech. Such success as I have had in the training of my horses is, therefore, merely a feeble homage to the revered memory of the former colonel of the 23RD *Dragoons, my first regiment.*

In explaining the results obtained, I have faithfully summarized the principles which have guided me, and it is quite natural, my dear General, in token of my lasting gratitude toward my last colonel, for me to beg the honor to dedicate to you my unassuming work on the horse—that noble animal which you have used so brilliantly—that valiant creature whose speed and courage enable us to surprise and conquer the enemy, as did you with the African Cavalry, "Surmounting all difficulties, crushing all resistance" in those supposedly inaccessible mountains athwart the Golesnitsa—Planina.

-Étienne BEUDANT.

PREFACE

For many years I have followed the work of Captain Beudant. I have been amazed at the marvelous results of his faultless method and am glad of this opportunity to express my appreciation. *"Extérieur et Haute École"* [*Outdoors and High School*] is written in a concise, attractive and agreeable style—as easy to read as a novel. It is a master's work that I should like to see in the hands of every horseman. It synthesizes all sense and logic ever written on the subject.

With his usual modesty, Captain Beudant disclaims having attempted anything except horse training during his tour of duty with the French Remount service in Morocco. However, it is an undeniable fact that the general improvement in conditions on Moroccan race-courses can be attributed to him only.

The story of his horses is a magnificent lesson and those who have had the rare pleasure of witnessing their exhibitions and seeing for themselves the perfection attained are filled with admiration.

A method must be judged by its results. Captain Beudant's horses, beautifully trained for outdoor work or in *haute école*, without restraint or fatigue, are living, visible proof of a method without fault.

He does not "break" the horse. Instead he makes of each lesson *a healthful exercise, an instructive game never continued to the point of fatigue.* He believes that errors most often occur in *attacking effects* instead of *destroying causes.*

To supple a horse, to teach him to respond to the slightest indication of hand or leg, to keep him good-tempered, to develop his natural qualities, to lead him on to amplify and exaggerate his action—this is true progress. We thus develop to the maximum all the ability and power of the horse, and require him to render all that he is capable of giving, without ever transgressing the limits of wholesome exercise.

Complete mastery of self, unlimited patience, firmness combined with kindness, keen observation, sure judgment, a faultless seat—all these Captain Beudant possesses to such a degree that errors are unknown in the training of his horses.

Lastly, his book is excellent because of the pains he has taken, before addressing those privileged horsemen capable of any phase of training, to show average horsemen a way, so simple to follow, so intelligible to the horse, as to insure success for both man and horse, however inept.

Captain Beudant's manual is the most systematic, the most practical, the most easily understood of all works on equitation. It will be read and re-read by all horsemen and riders—by all who love man's noblest companion.

Th. Monod,
Veterinaire principal de la premiere classe,
Director of Troop Veterinary Service,
Chief of Breeding,
French Remount Service in Morocco.

Introduction

FEARING just another book on horse training, I warily opened *"Extérieur et Haute École."* Its photographs were alluring. I had never seen horses worked in such freedom, or in their work, ridden with such ease and grace. Encouraged, I began reading and soon realized that I had come upon a writer who knew his subject; who had no difficult to comprehend, fantastic theories on training to expound; who went straight at his task, explained his method, and then proved it by results—his horses.

Captain Beudant disclaims any innovations, or new principles. He merely applies a few, simple old principles as their founders intended. These principles are generally known but little observed. The author's exposition of their application is novel, interesting and most convincing. He does not bother with petty detail, but focuses attention on the salient points of training. His is the correct ideal of a trained horse—one that seems to work completely free, meeting the demands of the moment as though unhampered by bit or rein.

At liberty the horse is always balanced, but when we mount we upset him. The object of intelligent training is merely to induce or to allow him to resume his natural balance. To be agreeable under the saddle he must be balanced; to be balanced he must be allowed freedom of movement. The center of gravity of a horse is constantly shifting; his balance ever changing. At the gallop, for instance, he is supported by three, two, or one foot, according to the phase of the stride, and there is also a moment of suspension when all feet are off the ground. Under these varying conditions he maintains his balance by employing his head and neck as a man in walking a rope employs a balance-pole. If denied the free use of his head and neck, he pulls, his gaits become rough; he stumbles or falls. The horse, not the rider, extricates the pair from difficulties. To get out of tight places, or over big fences he must have unrestricted use of his head and neck. No horse "choked" by his rider can have that "spare" leg so aptly described by Will Ogilvie[1]:

---

1   [William (Will) Abernethy Ogilvie, CM MBE (August 28, 1901-

"There is not the slightest doubt that when limbs
Were given out, the gods gave every gallant horse his share
Of a very useful four to employ in peace or war,
And another one to carry as a spare!"

To ride a horse skillfully is to train him—the only way to train him. A rider is as good as he rides; a method is no better than the man. A heavy-handed horseman, regardless of his knowledge, or method, cannot make an agreeable horse. The short, taut reins of the unskilled rider hurt the horse's mouth, and fetter his movements; he starts pulling, not for the pleasure of pulling, but in an attempt to escape pain and to regain freedom of movement. If we "hit" him on the mouth at one fence, or otherwise interfere with his jumping, he bolts, or refuses the next obstacle. He considers the interference intentional. Unfortunately we cannot apologize. To act when action is required; to permit the reins to slip to the end of the bight[2] when occasion demands; to sit still and do nothing when nothing is to be done—these are the marks of a horseman.

Captain Beudant's interpretation of the *haute école* is the best I have read. We Americans are little interested in this phase of riding. We are disposed to regard it as did a prince of the blood who, watching General L'Hotte in a private exhibition, exclaimed: "General, what patience you must have!" The old General gravely replied, "And a little skill too, Sire."

The French language is quite complete in the terminology of equitation; ours is very defective. To express in English the nuances of the French is difficult. I hope my feeble attempt will enable the reader at least to glimpse the picture the author has painted.

JOHN A. BARRY
TRANSLATOR
Lt. Col, U. S. Cavalry.
WASHINGTON, February 22, 1931.

1989) was a Canadian painter and war artist. In 1979, he was made a member of the Order of Canada. He was made a member of the Royal Canadian Academy of Arts. Editor's note]

2   Bight: the buckle or sewn seam where the ends of the reins are joined.

HORSE TRAINING: OUTDOOR AND HIGH SCHOOL

TRAINING

"The course of life runs not always as we have dreamed but rather as destiny decrees, and we should consider our duty done, our present task fulfilled when conscious of having done our best in the field of action flung by fate."
(GENERAL L'HOTTE)

WHILE on remount duty in Morocco, I tried "to do my bit" with horses. Lacking special aptitude for any department except that of equitation, I studied solely the training of the riding horse.

However, this subject is of prime importance, for it is well-known that both national economy and the efficiency of our cavalry require that horses be well-trained, without injury, and by a method that will prolong their service with the colors.

Moreover, it was frequently said before the war that *our equitation was inferior to that of the Germans.* So, having been unable to march to victory, as did real horsemen, I, a mere amateur, have undertaken to help destroy this heresy.

The result of my efforts has strengthened my convictions on the emptiness of theories and scientific formulae for the training of a riding horse.

The discourses on principles and the discussions about "effects of effects" are to me as "sounding brass or a tinkling cymbal." I firmly believe that *so long as the horse is not a soulless machine, so long as he enjoys mental faculties permitting him to receive impressions in all parts of his being more quickly than we can apply the aids deduced from our calculations, his training by the hard and fast rules of mathematics will ever remain the idle dream of a Utopian.*

I am convinced that the main requisites of training are: to observe the horse at liberty, to reflect, and to strive to perfect one's self rather than to blame the horse's unwillingness or imperfections.

The horse watches his rider and reacts to the movements that he makes, however slight or involuntary; then he reflects, and suddenly surprises the rider either by an unexpected defense or by the good execution of a movement which had been demanded of him in vain and which he has thought out while meditating in his stable.

It is certainly true, with few exceptions, that a good jumper whose rider is afraid of the obstacles very quickly ceases to jump. Also, a horse of which a gallop-depart has been asked but not obtained executes perfectly that same depart for the same rider the first time he is remounted even though a long time after the unsuccessful attempt.

To observe and *to reflect,* these are the rider's surest means of success.

Unfortunately for him, we usually blame the horse, and generally wrongly. In all probability he has responded to the aids actually applied and not to the aids we think we have applied. The fault is nearly always with the rider, who, not knowing how to speak the language of the aids correctly, has failed to make himself understood or has even expressed the exact opposite of what he wished to say.

The disability from which I suffer is a great handicap, but there is a bright side to everything and my inability to apply the aids strongly has been a great lesson to me. I can use but very little force, and the results obtained by my weak efforts have convinced me that horses are generally over-ridden; much more strength than necessary is habitually used in applying the aids.

The rider must reduce *his actions to the very minimum* and leave the horse *the greatest possible freedom in his.*

To be understood readily and quickly by the horse, the language of the aids must be the simplest, but in scientific theories it is rarely so, and the lessons are as difficult to give as to take. Training thus becomes as boring to the rider as to the horse. It is even said that in demanding a very simple movement, we must, for example, raise the right hand and carry that rein to the right; lower the left hand and close it on this rein; carry one leg forward, the other back; displace the seat to this or that side and incline the body to the front. Few of us can say to the horse so many things at one time without making a mistake and thus being misunderstood. I, for one, will not undertake such a task. I fear I might end raving.

Robersart II at the Passage, Captain Beudant up. Note the freedom of the horse, the ease and security of the rider.

It is also said that the aids must be applied at the precise moment at which this or that foot is raised or planted, etc., etc. In my humble opinion this is too exact and too exacting. A horse must not be robbed of his initiative. When I wish my horse to take the gallop, my aids acting on the horse's position imperceptibly put him into the gallop smoothly, without jerks and without any feeling or sensation other than that experienced when seated in a Pullman[3] which is smoothly started. It is only by the whir of the wheels that one realizes one is moving.

Finally, under the fallacy of improving on nature, the training methods of these scientists teach horses habits that are as awkward and troublesome to the horse as to the rider. These [so-called] master-horsemen, expending time and talent, finally succeed in getting a horse to make a descent of the neck[4] when a canter depart is demanded.

---

3   [Passenger car of a train. Editor's note.]

4   "*Descente d'encolure,*" "*descente de main,*" etc., are expressions used by some French horsemen and writers to indicate the action of a

"In peaceful calm reposing." Robersart II, Off a Bank in Morocco. Both Captain Beudant and his horse are perfectly at ease. Compare the positions of Robersart II's head and neck in jumping and in the *haute école* (see opposite).

At liberty, a horse never makes a descent of the neck, and mounted he does so only when cramped by the rider's hand, or when the rider believing in this utterly useless exercise has taught him the movement. Only very few horsemen obtain this movement, slowly and softly, and with the desired stretch of the neck, but they are the exceptions. The origin of this foolishness is generally heavy hands. The proof lies in the fact that the only way of correcting a horse of this bad habit is to stop cramping him—left free he quits the habit.

At Saumur I had read in a book by Captain Séyès, "depart at the gallop on a descent on the hand," and when as a sub-lieutenant I worked at equitation, I look great pains to obtain beautiful descents of the neck, very gently executed, But never being able to understand the efficacy of this tiresome exercise, I quit it, and since then my first care always has been to cure this habit when found in horses entrusted to me. Furthermore, I must say that,

---

horse, at the call of the rider, in gently and softly stretching and lowering his neck and head, with the lower jaw mobile. These expressions have been translated "descent of the neck" and "descent *on* [or *of*] the hand." Translator's note.

From a photograph copyright by Harris & Ewing.
On and Off a Truck. Major-General Guy V. Henry, Chief of Cavalry,
U. S. A.

with the exception of my first chargers, I have never ridden any horse that made descents of the neck slowly and gently.

About 1902 or 1903, in studying the method of General Faverot de Kerbrech, I read therein this suggestion: "Have the horse execute as many descents on the hands and legs as possible." I did not know what to think, for the descent on the hand, as I understood it, was contrary to the constant search for that lightness in which there is no bobbing of the head. I decided to write to the General, who immediately sent me the following explanation: "Descent on the hands and legs means simply the complete and absolute cessation of their action and feel on the horse. In other words, leave the horse completely free as long as he maintains the correct position, gait, and speed. This is proof that the horse is truly in balance."

This explanation pleased me greatly, for the descent on the hand, as thus understood, corresponded to the ideal I was striving for in training—an ideal obtained from observing horses at liberty in America and Africa.

Balance is the goal to seek. It is also the stumbling block of calculators who try to TEACH equestrian art by theory. Indeed, as early as 1776 Dupaty de Clam, a musketeer of the olden times, wrote in his thesis at the Academy of Sciences, Literature, and Arts at Bordeaux:

> "But one cannot hope to TEACH this tact and delicate discernment which come only from practice. The art consists of a singular skill and a genius, unimagined, much less appreciated, by those who do not frequently practice it, little observed by many who do, and often neglected entirety by great scholars. Marvelous and ravishing when seen by knowing eyes, the field is limitless, and the classic authors, had they devoted volumes to the subject, could not thereby have produced a single horseman."

METHODS

"Let us not depend too much on science. Study, rather, the laws of nature, habitually correct in her work; meditate upon them, and with nature as our guide, we shall arrive more surely at our goal."
(ROUSSELET)

When it comes to practice, few rules are absolute. Admittedly there are principles. It takes blue and yellow to make green, but it is tact and genius that enable the artist to show the *nuance* of wavelets and the gentle zephyrs of woods and prairie. So it is with the rules of equitation.

The rider must find and adopt the method best suited to his ability. He must study the temperament of the horse to be trained, for temperament differs in individuals, and a principle, in its application, varies with temperament. A horse must be suppled, and once suppled, *regardless of the means,* he responds to any aid that is logical, and judiciously applied, provided he is not asked to respond to a form of special training, for example, to halt when the spur is applied in front of the girth and to go forward when it is applied to the rear.

Actually, in riding a trained horse, we use at each instant and intuitively, according to needs, the aids in different ways; at one time diagonal aids[5], at another, lateral. Tact directs us.

But with an untrained horse we must proceed methodically. To obtain a certain result, we must always use the same aids in the same manner; otherwise we confuse and excite the horse. We must never lose sight of the fact that an excited horse is, in a measure, insane; maddened by hunger, he throws the oats from the manger in his hurry to get at them; crazed by thirst, he grabs the water-bucket and spills the water. *To understand, he must be calm.*

Many training methods claim superiority; apparently they are quite different, actually they are founded on the same basic principles. All precepts come from the teachings of Baucher

---

5   For example, the right hand and left leg used together are "diagonal aids," the right hand and right leg used together are "lateral aids."—*Translator's note.*

and Comte d'Aure[6], the two great masters of the modern art of equitation. The principles of these two pioneers are the same, and it is regrettable that their respective partisans have striven harder to exaggerate their differences than to learn the causes of the disagreements between the two schools. A reconciliation of these disagreements would lead to a practical method of training horses and would save a lot of horse flesh.

Comte d'Aure taught that the horse should go forward at the call of the legs, and more or less on the hands, according to his intended use. Baucher maintained that the horse should be behind the hands, in front of the legs and continually striving to increase his collection by raising his head and neck and getting his haunches farther under him.

Comte d'Aure put impulsion first of all, and was continually ordering his pupils *"En avant"* (Forward); Baucher, who was forever seeking lightness, constantly repeated *"Poussez"* (Drive with your legs).

General L'Hotte[7] said that both Baucher and Comte d'Aure put impulsion first of all, but Baucher, instead of allowing it to escape immediately in forward movement, wanted the rider first to master it in order to obtain more complete control over the efforts of the horse. These teachings, greatly distorted by endless discussions, have formed sects and produced interminable and useless arguments.

Comte d'Aure rejected the use of force and wanted the horse placed in a position to act for himself; he did not seek complete possession of the animal's forces. He sought relative lightness only. Baucher, with the flowering of his genius, inspired by horses at liberty, obtained a natural balance in which the horse, as light to

---

6   Comte d'Aure and Baucher, contemporaries and great rivals, revolutionized riding on the continent of Europe. Before their time (the nineteenth century) the training doctrines of the old Versailles school were followed. Comte d'Aure stressed the training essential for a good "outside" horse; Baucher's *forte* was the *"haute école."*—*Translator's note.*

7   A distinguished officer of French cavalry. A pupil of both Comte d'Aure and Baucher, and one of the greatest horsemen that ever lived.—*Translator's note.*

legs as to hands, seemed to move and work spontaneously. He demanded and got complete possession of the horse. He arrived at complete and perfect lightness. His was the refinement, the very pinnacle of the equitation of Comte d'Aure but it was the same equitation.

In my opinion, the only true formula to adopt is that of General L'Hotte: "To have the horse sensitive and light to the legs as well as to the hands, that is to say: to have him always flowing between the legs, yet unseizable by them unless the hands oppose the forward movement."

To train a horse, the experts of the different schools of training develop some very ingenious theories and attempt to prove the necessity for their difficult application by learned demonstrations frequently backed up by figures and calculations in mechanics.

Sometimes I admire those horsemen who really believe in these scientific principles, but I have never dared follow them in their studies, which are much too deep for me. Moreover, I am certain that it is their claims and pretensions that have called forth such harsh criticisms on our equestrian instruction, on the poor training of our cavalry horses, and their premature breakdown in service. A training system, it seems to me, must consider the moral qualities of the horse and not seek to force him to coordinate his efforts exactly with the laws of mechanics. The horse should be the master, not the slave, of these laws.

The understanding of a horseman comes from his heart, not from mathematical calculations. Why then try to make of his noble comrade a mere automaton? What purpose then serves his magnificent courage, that quality we prize most, whether on race track or in the hunting field—wherever he serves—in traces or under saddle?

D'Auvergne[8], the "father" of military equitation, said: "To devote one's self only to the artistic side of riding is foolish; the practical side, based on correct principles, must not be neglected."

---

8   Henri de la Tour d'Auvergne, Vicomte de Turenne, often called simply Turenne (11 September 1611, Sedan, Ardennes–27 July 1675) *Editor's note.*

There are two ways of appealing to the moral nature of a horse:
1. by terrifying him;
2. the other, by speaking logically through the medium of the aids to his intelligence.

Fillis[9], in his book on equitation, says: "There always comes a time (in training) when the horse plays his last card and fights in desperation. As long as a horse is unconquered, his training is incomplete."

A struggle always leaves its mark on the spirit or the body of the horse. If it does not make him stubborn it is likely to damage his legs.

The ill-treated horse first gets excited, then, especially if a nervous type, he becomes maddened and exasperated, and the greater his exasperation the less he understands. Finally, he stands with all four feet firmly planted, all muscles contracted. I cannot imagine how, in such a condition, he can be brought to reason by continuing the abuse.

It is calmness, and nothing else, which converts disordered jerky gaits into smooth, flowing ones. Here is one very important phase of training in which there must be no struggle. **A teacher must first get the *confidence* of his pupil, then reveal the presence of *kindness, gentleness and a will, that though calm, is inflexible.*** This is the immutable and sovereign law of teaching, whether the pupil is man or beast.

To others more skillful, I leave the doctrine of violence. I have not the strength to practice it even if I wished. I merely try my best to follow the gentler rule of General Faverot de Kerbrech: "For the horse as for the rider, the lesson should be a healthful exercise, an instructive game, never prolonged to the point of fatigue. When sweat appears the rider has gone too far."

A spoiled horse, made stubborn by harsh treatment, sometimes has a bad disposition—an unbroken horse, never. **I am convinced that the first requisite of a successful trainer is a complete realization that he is not infallible.** To think that he must be the Devil himself is vanity, opposed alike to good training,

---

9   James Fillis (1834-1913) was a well-known English-born French riding master.

A French Officer.
The horse, in complete freedom, is using his head and neck to the maximum.

to the soundness of the horse, and to the instruction of the rider. It is much easier to use force than brains. When after careful observation one is almost certain that his actions have been logical, his demands intelligent and intelligible, and that he has not violated involuntarily the simple laws of mechanics by weighting a member that should have been lightened, or committed any similar error; then, when the horse continues to disobey, instead of punishing, it is much better to regain his confidence, induce him to relax, and try again to make him obey. I insist that a horse habitually responds logically to demands made upon him. Instead then of trying to force him to respond to our possibly and, indeed, probably illogical or unintelligible demands, we had better *carefully study ourselves.* The correctness of the response is almost *always in proportion* to the accuracy of the demand. If the horse does not obey, the rider has only himself to blame; he may not have given the horse the correct position or sufficient impulsion to comply with his demands, or he may have been guilty of any one or many of the countless sins of omission and commission.

"In summary, it is by mild, timely action, always anticipating and blocking defenses, that the horse is taught obedience." (Rousselet)

By the constant application of these principles the horse becomes gentle and willing, and his education is facilitated in proportion to the trainer's adherence to the wise observation of General Faverot de Kerbrech:

> "In training there is always the tendency to proceed too rapidly. [In order] to arrive quickly, go slowly with careful, cautious steps. Make frequent demands; be content with little; be lavish with rewards."

If one hasn't the benefit of a good instructor, one must study and analyze the recognized works on equitation; borrow and adopt from them the rules best suited to one's aptitude and purpose. Unfortunately, and to my great embarrassment, I admit that I have found these works complicated, too learned, too esoteric, too difficult to digest. For instance, I have not had the courage to learn the analysis of the gaits, and when I read: "In acting with this leg at that moment, the raising of the horse's right foot is quickened, etc., etc."; "To take the gallop with the right lead, the horse's croup must be pushed to the right for such and such a reason"—I find it too much for me, and I skip to another page or close the old book.

When I see in a course of training prescribed for noncommissioned officers that the rider *must count the gallop strides;* that he must pull on one rein at this stride and on another at that, I am amazed and say to myself, "It must be very difficult to ride a horse according to these rules, and in these new times I'd be a very poor corporal."

I have had only one riding instructor, Lieutenant Champion, at Saumur, who later commanded the remount depot at Montrouge, and died gloriously in battle early in the war. He was a bold rider and the only advice he ever gave was, *"Tirez dessus, tapez dedans."*[10]

---

10   The exact meaning is difficult, if not impossible, to render in English. As used here its approximate meaning is "Push 'em and pull 'em."—*Translator's note.*

After thirty-five years of continuous study I've come to believe he was right. All training resolves itself into teaching a horse to obey the hands and to go forward at the call of the legs. The rest is imagination.

At Saumur I read part of the book by Captain Séyès explaining the method of Major Dutilh. Unfortunately I got nothing from the book and returned it to its owner.

In 1898 I glanced over James Fillis'[11] book. Its pictures charmed me and to this day I regret that I did not have the opportunity to study it carefully. If memory serves, James Fillis wrote in substance, and very truly, that there was no more cause for astonishment at seeing a horse making the prodigious efforts required in some airs of the *haute école* than at seeing a gymnast executing his *tours de force*. Rational exercises make the muscles of the horse, as well as those of the gymnast, capable of stretching to their extreme limit without breaking.

In 1915, at Rabat I came across Captain de Saint-Phalle's book[12] (1st edition). In it I read beneath an illustration, as I remember, that the mare Mademoiselle d'Etiolles was ridden in a special bridle, permitting the use of one bit or another according to the high school air demanded. That was enough for me, and fearing scientific discussion I closed the book. Afterwards I was ashamed and felt that my laziness was unpardonable, until a few months later I learned that Captain de Saint-Phalle, in riding his horses, played, without ever suspecting it, on instruments horribly out of tune, and that all of them, save perhaps Marseille II, were very stubborn even when he was in the saddle. This wrecks all that Captain de Saint-Phalle tried to build, for tractability is unquestionably an indispensable quality in the riding horse whose most important role is *work out-of-doors.* It must never be forgotten that the supplings of the *manège* and *haute école* are only a veneer

---

11   James Fillis, a master horseman. Died early in twentieth century. His book, *"Principes de Dressage et d'Equitation'* which Clemenceau, the Tiger, helped him write, is well-known in the United States under the title of "Breaking and Riding,"—*Translator's note.*

12   Captain Jacques Marquis de Saint-Phalle [1867-1908], *Dressage et Emploi du Cheval de Selle*, Paris, A. Legoupy, [1899].

of useful elegance, not absolutely necessary in a system of training intended merely to produce an agreeable outdoor horse.

The test of a real horseman is his ability to manage his horse; to suppress all resistances due to lack of training or to stubbornness. What then are we to think of complicated principles by which we occasionally obtain, it is true, some airs, more or less bizarre, but which do not teach us how to take our horse WHERE WE WISH, WHEN WE WISH, AS WE WISH.

The book of Captain de Saint-Phalle confirms my conviction on the futility of all mechanical theories difficult to apply, and it proves that we must always come back to Rousselet's conclusion:

> "Study rather the laws of nature, habitually correct in her work; meditate upon them, and with nature as our guide we shall arrive more surely at our goal."

We must remember that the truly great masters, instead of having stubborn horses, astonished their audiences not only with the brilliance and willingness of their mounts, but also by their ability to ride and the ease with which they were able to manage seemingly impossible and incorrigible horses. These great masters have, likewise, never been charged that they employed special instruments for the various movements demanded; nor did they divide equitation into that of the school (*manège*) and that of the out-of-doors; nor have they made a distinction between transverse and longitudinal balance; nor concerned themselves with any other such things.

D'Absac provoked the exclamation; "You are either the Devil or M. D'Absac!"

Rousselet rode always triumphantly and easily the horses his pupils could not manage.

Comte d'Aure aroused the enthusiasm of the most exacting horsemen of his day by easily managing vicious horses upon which some celebrated amateurs, Lord Seymour and others, put him to the test. At the same time d'Aure rode, with a brilliance then unknown, the handsome stallions from the Stud at Le Pin and performed marvels with his schooled horses, notably with his favorite, Le Cerf.

As to Baucher, who next to General L'Hotte was *the greatest equestrian genius that ever lived*—the majority of his horses were vicious brutes before he owned and trained them. For example, Kléber who no one could ride on account of his viciousness, bad gaits, and lack of strength, became an extraordinary product of the *haute école*, after only a very short time under Baucher's training.

"Kléber was a stallion," writes General L'Hotte, "and in the vicinity of mares was prone to become greatly excited, but between the legs of his master he did not notice them at all."

Many other such instances could be cited, but the following, which I think is the most striking, must suffice: the case of Gericault. General L'Hotte tells the story:

> "One evening at the circus, Baucher had just received his usual enthusiastic welcome, when Lord Seymour remarked that he had a three-year-old, Gericault, that Baucher with all his skill and science could not ride through the Bois de Boulogne. M. de Lancosme Brèves accepted the challenge, saying there was no need to trouble the master with such a matter; that he would ride the colt himself. M. de Lancosme Brèves won the bet—Gericault was the stake—and then courteously gave the colt to Baucher."

To ride the horse through the Bois was evidence of the skill of M. de Lancosme Brèves, but more remarkable was the fact that Baucher rode the savage beast twenty-four hours later, in full circus, surrounded by crowds and lights, and frightened by the thunderous applause the master always received. He not only rode him, but put him through the airs of the *haute école*.

I have never had the honor, even at Saumur, of taking part in a *reprise,* or a *séance* of the *haute école.* However, I have often had the good fortune to admire, with the most jealous attention, some officers whose horses will forever remain in my memory as the ideal of which an amateur may dream. In my opinion, nothing can compare in gaits with the horses I've seen General Faverot de Kerbrech gallop, with those of Colonel de Bauchêne at Lunéville, with those of Colonel Coutades under whom I served in Algiers—or with many of the horses trained by Colonel Communal, who had me ride them when he was a lieutenant at Constantine and Miliana, and a captain at Tiaret.

The greatest pleasure to be got from horses is to gallop a well-trained one over varied country, dotted here and there with jumps, and I cannot understand why anyone would try to obtain the more or less stiff and fantastic airs of the school before making an agreeable and pleasant outdoor horse. If I have often done the contrary it has been because circumstances forced me to it: either the unsuitable country in which I was stationed or the lack of quality in my horses that could, at most, merely serve in studying the *haute école*.

When I was in a plaster cast I read the lighter parts, the easiest reading, of Gustave Le Bon's book, *L'Équitation Actuelle*. In my most humble opinion, this work is the Utopia of a learned psychologist who has conceived it his duty to praise to the skies German equitation, especially that of Plenzier, *"Écuyer en Chef"* to the German Emperor. The author even tries to show that in the posting trot as practiced in England, France and elsewhere, the body should be vertical rather than inclined to the front and that the stirrups should be lengthened, not shortened.

Nevertheless, a great *master* of the French school—a master by order it is true—has expressed his enthusiasm for *L'Équitation Actuelle,* and goes so far as to compare it to the shining light St. Paul saw on the road to Damascus!

From a philosophical and mathematical view point and also from the view point of the principles discussed, the book is perfect. Indeed, the methods of the great masters, of whom Comte d'Aure and Baucher are representative, could not be more aptly summarized than by Le Bon when he states:

> "The legs create impulsion; the hands prescribe the manner in which it is to be expended."

He also says:

> "The reasoned training of a horse is a mental gymnastic, builds character in the rider, in a way that no theoretical instruction can replace. It teaches him firmness, kindness, and patience, and greatly develops his judgment and powers of observation. In [the process

Signor Alvisi, Italy
A prominent exhibitor in European jumping classes, and point-to-points.

of] training a horse, a man also trains himself, and this training he will find useful in various walks of life. I know of no more useful complement of education than training a horse. Professional psychologists, if they tried it, would be surprised at the many things they would learn. It is a broad field for research, still unexplored and awaiting them."

Some of his other ideas are debatable, for instance:

"The horse always reflects by his obedience, by his resistance or hesitation, by the perfection or imperfection of his training, the character of his rider. Generally it is not difficult to diagnose a man's character after riding a horse he has trained."

I would say, rather, that we can at least determine the nature and character of his talent.
From the view point of training, Le Bon's reasoning

is logical, but his premises are usually false. Here are some examples:

1. "The work of the *haute école* nearly always produces a short base of support because it tends to shorten the gaits." True, the basic exercise for the *haute école*, the *piaffer*[13], is a gait in which the horse's movements are short, but at the same time, the piaffe supples the joints and greatly develops the muscles of the croup. The *passage*[14] is likewise an excellent preparation for a brilliant trot; the most beneficial of all the airs of the *haute école* is the Spanish trot[15], for nothing else so develops the play of the shoulders—shoulder-mobility—as does this beautiful air of fantasy.

2. "The horse at liberty knows well how to manage his affairs, but with a rider in the saddle, his gaits become unnatural, that is to say, irregular, and it is for the trainer to regularize them."

Everyone who has watched horses move in open country at liberty, or under riders making no effort to balance them, or even when used as pack animals, is amazed at their cleverness and skill. A horse ridden in a halter or with nothing at all on his head is always straight and his gaits are regular. Usually it is otherwise when the rider attempts to guide or balance him. Le Bon himself tells of a time in the Indies, on a narrow mountain trail along which he was riding faster than he wished, when he owed his safety entirely to his horse, which he left on his own and made no attempt to guide. I am sure that horse had regular gaits.

The truth is that skill may rectify gaits which have been spoiled by man and become habitual with a horse controlled by the rider's aids; but it was obedience to these aids that ruined the gaits.

---

13 A collected gait in which the horse executes a high trot in place—without advancing. It is explained later by the author.—*Translator's note.*

14 The *piaffer* advancing.—*Translator's note.*

15 A trot in which the horse extends the forelegs to a horizontal position.—*Translator's note.*

3. "How are we to make him obey us?" asks Gustave Le Bon, and he answers: "by immediately rewarding each obedience and punishing each disobedience."

Here, he enunciates a principle to which, though correct in itself, are due nearly all the failures in training, for almost always the horse tries his best to respond to orders which in most instances are poorly expressed. The rider alone is to blame, yet he punishes a horse that has done what he *was actually asked to do*.

It is not only a question of deciding the method to use in obtaining a certain movement from a horse placed on the aids as we wish him, it is also a question of modifying the method to suit the circumstances of the moment. The horse carries our weight [the rider's] and his own, which, together change the balance and the horse therefore instinctively feels, much more accurately than we do, HOW and WHEN the formula should be modified. This is why the horse must be left free to dispose of his forces [strength] as he sees fit, so as to obtain the results that we are seeking.

But far be it from me to dispute with learned horsemen their ability to apply their calculation and formulae. I readily admit and repeat it, that it is beyond me and that I am utterly incapable of using at the same time the four aids plus one or two displacements of the seat to obtain a simple canter-depart which the horse, left to himself, knows how to take much better and more gracefully than when cramped by mechanical preparations which set him oblique to his direction of travel.

I must say, that instead of emphasizing more and more the schooling exercises, I have come to the conclusion that shoulder-in and two-track[16] work are nothing more than amusing diversions,

---

16   A horse is said to go on "two tracks" when his fore and hind legs follow different tracks. In "shoulder-in" the horse, slightly and uniformly bent from poll to croup, continues his direction of travel thus bent. He really goes on two trucks. "Shoulder-in" is highly valued by most horsemen as a suppling exercise for the horse. In addition to the general idea conveyed, the phrase "on two tracks" also means a particular movement in which the horse straight from poll to croup travels oblique to his original direction [leg-yeild].—*Translator's note.*

often detrimental to the horse, and of utility only in permitting the mounted soldier to place his horse properly in ranks.

I have never seen a horse at liberty swing [displace] his haunches to one side in order to break into a natural gait, trot, gallop, or *passage.* Therefore, it is illogical to compel him to cross his legs when mounted.[17] Briefly, *all training is this and nothing more:* **the spurs to provoke action; the bridoon to direct the action that produces the movement.**[18]

I never traverse a horse except through a whim or in order not to go contrary to the established custom. On the contrary, when I am teaching a horse to trot, gallop or *passage,* or to change legs at the gallop, I never cease in my efforts to keep him as straight as possible from shoulders to croup.

Two masters have been my guides: one, General Faverot de Kerbrech in his *"Dressage Methodìque du Cheval de Selle a'apres les derniers enseignments de Baucher"* [*Methodical Dressage of the Riding Horse According to Baucher's Last Teachings*, Xenophon Press, 2010]; the other, General L'Hotte in his *Un Officier de Cavalerie* ("An Officer of Cavalry") in which, instead of presenting a method or system of training, General L'Hotte cites principles, and explains the application of those principles by various masters.

General L'Hotte, a pupil worthy of his two great teachers, Comte d'Aure and Baucher, was the foremost horseman of his day. Some of L'Hotte's horses were superior even to Baucher's and he [General L'Hotte] was known as "the incomparable Horseman."

In L'Hotte's book, which I cannot console myself for having lost though I have saved numerous notes, he says he trained some of his horses according to the method of Comte d'Aure, others were trained according to Baucher. Later in his exposition of the work of these horses—the way they did it—he convinced me that the bases of the methods of these two great, masters were identical.

---

17   Most riders, in putting a horse into a left lead canter, for example, push his haunches to the left. Here, the author is arguing against that practice.—*Translator's note.*

18   *éperons pour provoquer l'action, bridon pour diriger l'action qui produit le movement.*

They sought the same end but to a different degree. Each sought impulsion and lightness.

Baucher, to mediocre riders, recommends the alternate rather than the simultaneous employment of the aids so as to simplify their action and to avoid errors resulting from lack of their accord[19].

General Faverot de Kerbrech has taken for the base of his method this doctrine, "Hands without legs, legs without hands," and says that it must be followed unless there is a real reason for acting otherwise. But he distinctly states:

> "There comes a time in training and later in the management of a trained horse, when the effects of the legs must be united to those of the hands. This comes about very naturally and without danger of lack of accord, because the training has then reached the point where application of the aids is a mere *nuance*."

With Comte d'Aure the horse is always on the bit—but. negligibly so—by the weight of the reins only, when he is light to leg and hand.

The book of General Faverot de Kerbrech [*Methodical Dressage of the Riding Horse, Xenophon Press, 2010*], I believe, is the only one, (James Fillis' excepted,) which tries to instruct the reader—to really teach him—instead of parading a science whose secrets remain jealously guarded. It does not deal with theories; consequently it is simple, clear, and any one can understand this most practical of all methods. This is why we owe so much to General Faverot de Kerbrech. He summarized the last teachings of the great Baucher of whom General L'Hotte said:

---

19   The hands are the superior or upper aids; the legs are the inferior or lower aids. It is easier to use just one set [of aids] at a time; there is less chance for confusion, that is to say of the hands contradicting the legs or vice versa (lack of accord [between the driving and the directing aids]). Therefore to mediocre riders, which most of us are, Baucher recommended "Hands without legs, legs without hands."—*Translator's note*.

Point-to-Point at Pau.
Baron La Caze on the clean-bred Monsieur-Printemps.

"It is to him more than any other that La Bruyère's words apply: 'When one excels in an art, be it what it may, and develops that art to the most exquisite perfection, he exalts it to the realm of the noblest and best.'"

Hands Without Legs, Legs Without Hands

Amateurs will act wisely in limiting themselves as I do, to a simple method, within reach of all, and which may be thus summarized: When impulsion is produced by the legs, the hands must limit their action to directing or retaining it. In this way we avoid confusing the horse and make it easy for him to understand, because the legs are always used to push the horse to the front; the hands act in the opposite sense, unless they are used to indicate a definite direction of travel without which the horse would become confused. In other words, legs for forward movement; hands for rearward and sideward movements.

When legs and hands are used simultaneously, the legs instinctively correct blunders of the hands, and vice versa; the rider is unaware of his mistakes. On the contrary, their alternate use deprives the rider of these instinctive and reciprocal corrections.

"Errors then become evident," says General L'Hotte, "and the rider soon learns that he himself frequently provokes resistance by using too much or not enough force; he nearly always uses too much, and in general, the less the better. The best plan is to use a *minimum of force* and that in such a way as not to confuse the horse."

Therefore an inexpert rider should adopt the method of alternate use of hands and legs. Particularly, hands and legs should never be used simultaneously on an untrained horse. On the other hand, in the management of a well-trained horse, it is often necessary to unite the effects of hands and legs.

Definitions

TACT: The genius of equitation—the feel of the horse. It is the gauge by which the rider knows HOW, WHEN, HOW MUCH and HOW LONG to act. With tact, the rider gets out of difficulties and succeeds.

AIDS: The aids transmit the rider's will to the horse. They are the hands, the legs, spurs, whip, clucks, and displacement of the seat.

The displacement of the seat, to which the horse is extremely sensitive, should be avoided except in a full gallop. It is very difficult to displace the seat accurately and correctly, especially in movements quickly repeated, such us changes of leg at the canter with the same number of strides between changes. These displacements worry the horse to a greater or lesser extent and are certainly very awkward and ungraceful. Two exceptions are sometimes allowable: when the rider pushes his buttocks under him and bears down with his seat to drive the horse forward; also a forward inclination of the rider's body aids the horse in backing. With these exceptions, we must never forget that the most important consideration is *aplomb*[20], always *aplomb*.

IMPULSION: Force at the horse's disposition which propels him always as the rider directs. Impulsion is the indispensable element in the employment of the horse in the *haute école* as well as out-of-doors.

> "It is the wind which fills the sails of the boat... With impulsion as with steam, the rider handles the throttle and puts on or shuts off steam at his will, but always smoothly." (Comte d'Aure.)

Impulsion is keenness, and a horse is finished, is agreeable to ride cross-country, in the park, in the school and in the *haute école* only when he has impulsion; only when he is keen. Make no mistake, impulsion is not a defense which the horse adopts at his whim or fancy to take advantage of his rider in a dangerous way. In the riding horse, it is only the force that grows only as much as required by the execution of the movement saught.

Cross-country, impulsion makes a horse take just a nice feel of the bit; or said another way, his feel on the bit never attempts to surpass the support of the hands, which may very well be a simple contact.

This contact between the mouth of the horse and the hand increases at faster gaits; at speed it becomes firm enough to give confidence to the rider, and boldness to the horse. At the slower gaits it is reduced to the mere weight of the reins, and during the descent of the hand and leg, the horse maintains his own balance.

---

20   Imperturbable self-possession, poise, or assurance. The perpendicular, or vertical, position.

ACTION: That is to say, impulsion emanating' from the s p i r i t of the horse is a quality which man's violence may i n c i t e, but like the noble ambition of a soldier, it cannot exist without self-respect.

The force communicated to the horse through the rider's aids, be they ever so powerful and skilled, is negligible—powerless to engender speed on the flat, or courage in front of big fences. In the *haute école* it leads inevitably to the painful execution of some airs, the *passage* for example, where the haunches dolefully drag along under the shriveling effects of the rider's legs. On the other hand, when the horse works for sport, as he thinks, the energy he displays is marvelous. The sportive cooperation of the horse is the key to success on the track, in horse shows, cross-country and lastly in the *haute école.* At the *passage,* the most brilliant of airs, it is only when the horse is working free, for the sheer joy of living, that we get the rhythmic and rounded hock-action, the smooth, elastic play of muscles, the lordly carriage of head and tail—incomparable gestures, investing him with a majesty that demands admiration.

ACTION is a psychological phenomenon beyond the calculations of mathematics. To attempt to build a system of equitation based on mathematical formulae is merely building castles in the air.

POSITION: Is the distribution of weight upon the horse's four legs as required by the demands of the [particular] movement. It is supplemented by a disposition of forces to suit this distribution of weight.

MOVEMENT: Is the effect of action on position. Conversely, the transition from movement to inaction is the effect of position on action.

At liberty, at the walk or gallop, the horse stretches his neck and carries it almost horizontally, especially when doing his best at these gaits; at the trot he slightly raises the head and neck; but when he is "on parade" and showing himself in all his splendor, his entire carriage is loftier; the neck is as high as possible, the forehead is vertical or nearly so.

I think the best position for the horse when mounted is the one he would assume at liberty if he were executing the movements demanded by the rider. This is my sole disagreement with General Faverot de Kerbrech who wanted the forehead fixed constantly at the vertical. I am not completely confident of being right. I am simply following through with my idea of imitating nature.

BALANCE: "A horse mounted is balanced when the rider, by the merest suggestion, can modify the distribution of weight among the four bases [legs] of support." (General Faverot de Kerbrech)

At liberty, the horse is always balanced. In other words, his weight is correctly distributed upon his four supports and he modifies this distribution in accordance with the requirements of the moment. Consequently, it is logical to allow him when mounted all possible freedom. The ideal is a horse who, at the slightest indication from his rider, acts aidlessly; who maintains his balance himself; and who appears to go as he likes, even in the airs of the *haute école.* Outdoors, or in cross-country, he gallops as the wild horse, jumping banks, ditches or whatever bars his way. To approximate this ideal it is logical to proceed as we do with the education of a person. Above all, avoid provoking the pupil's dislike for the work at hand; on the contrary, interest him in the work, but if necessary show him by means that are firm yet without roughness that he must obey.

The heaviest headed brute of a squadron is surprisingly agile when at liberty. Then why is he so awkward and clumsy when mounted? Not, as is so widely believed, because of the rider's weight, since he minds that little except on long tiresome outings. The true reason for his pitiable figure and awkwardness is the rider's opposition to the horse's balance. The rider does not [always] allow the horse to make a natural disposition of his weight; it is on account of the rider that the horse stiffens all over and loses his faculties, just exactly as fear is the cause of man's inability to swim spontaneously as all other animals do. From colthood, horses passage, change leads at the canter, and jump without difficulty, but when we mount them they do not even know how to walk.

Major Cole, U.S.A.
If a fault were to be made at this jump, it
must be scored against the horse, and not the rider.

The preceding discussion, I think, shows conclusively that training a horse consists of: gaining his confidence, suppling his all of his muscles, and of inducing him to place all his forces at the disposition of the rider so that the rider may make use of those he needs, or according to circumstances, *it allow the horse to use them as he sees fit.*

Movement and balance are inseparable. This is a fundamental of training. Baucher expressed it as follows:

> "Balance must be obtained without distorting the movement, and conversely, movement, while in operation, must leave balance undisturbed."

BEHIND THE AIDS[21]: "A horse is behind the aids [literally: cornered] whenever his forces are behind the rider's legs." (Baucher)

The state of being behind the bit must not be confused with rein-back, which is a regular, free and easy movement to the

---

21   *Acculement*

rear. In rein-back properly done, the horse is not behind the rider's legs; their slightest action carries the horse immediately forward again.

TO SEPARATE THE FORCE [POWER] AND THE MOVEMENT: In training, whenever balance is lost or serious resistance appears, power [force] and movement must be separated. To do this, leave the horse inactive until his balance is reestablished, until no trace of the movement which provoked the [forceful] defense remains in his system. When calm is restored the rider again puts the horse into action and places him in the *position* calculated to produce the movement sought or the gait that was interrupted.

THE STRAIGHT HORSE: The greatest difficulty in equitation is to keep the horse straight—straight from shoulders to croup. Our efforts to keep the horse straight are usually illogical. To straighten a horse we should act on his FOREHAND not on his HINDQUARTERS[22]. If the haunches are carried to the left, a right indirect rein will straighten the horse by putting his shoulders in line. The use of the leg on the side toward which he carries the haunches will not suffice; furthermore, when that leg's action ceases, the haunches will return to the out-of-line position. On the contrary, the indirect rein is easy to use and assures success. The reason is simple. Traversed haunches [displaced to one side] are caused by faulty distribution of weight on the shoulders. If, instead of trying to eradicate the effect, we destroy the cause,

---

22   In reading this or any other accurate work on riding, the reader should constantly keep in mind the following: A horse gets out of line, and hence unbalanced, because he has failed to maintain the proper distribution of weight over his bases of support [four legs]. Examples: If he over-weights the forehand; result—he becomes heavy in hand, he pulls. If he over-weights the right fore leg; the result is that the haunches which are lightened, go to the left because a horse follows this excess of weight. In the last case an over-weighted right foreleg tends to cause him to turn to right and, with shoulders turning right, his haunches go to the left.
   The author is making the point that the haunches being out of alignment is the effect of over-weighting one shoulder. His advice is to address the cause and not the effect.—*Translator's note.*

the [undesirable] effect will disappear; and the horse will be straightened.

A horse's habit of getting out of alignment, of not remaining straight, always comes from poor t r a i n i n g and from the annoyance of an unskilled rider. Even good riders rarely produce perfectly straight horses; on the other hand, the horses in Arabian countries when ridden by uneducated natives without saddle, bridle or halter are invariably absolutely straight. But, when those same natives, imagining themselves horsemen, use bridles, saddles and spurs, these same horses are never straight; they invariably travel traversed—as a dog travels.

SUPPORT REIN[23]: From the principle, "hands to direct and to retain, legs to drive forward," follows naturally the use of the support rein. Thus, to move or pass the horse on two tracks to the right; the right leg first provides the necessary impulsion, then the left leg pushes the haunches, and the left rein pushes the shoulders to the right. If [by common mistake] only the right rein is used, the muzzle will be pulled to the right, and the weight of the neck will stay back on left shoulder, which then [being overloaded] is unable follow [to the right], making the movement very difficult[24].

DIAGONAL EFFECTS: If the bow of a boat is pulled to the right and its stern pushed to the right, it is clear that the entire boat will move to the right and remain parallel[25] to its original direction, but with reference to what has just been said of the supportive

---

23   *rêne d'appui* [uni-lateral aids are described here, to effect the leg-yield; in this example left leg and left rein applied after the right leg provides impulsion. Also described is the common mistake of pulling the horse to the wall with the right rein, which leads to inferior results.—*Editor's note*]

24   Again, the principle of the horse following his weight applies. In this assumed case this principle is violated.—*Translator's note.*

25   Provided always, that the pull and push are properly coordinated.—*Translator's note.*

rein, this is not the case with the horse. Since a boat is rigid, but the horse is flexible, if his head would be pulled and his haunches pushed, both to the right, the left shoulder being over-weighted by the bend in the neck [created by pulling the right rein], the horse comes behind the aids, the left foreleg which should exceed the right, instead remains backward, [to the left], it is overweighted by the weight of the neck. In addition, the right rein cramps the freedom of the right shoulder. The diagonal effects, which tend to teach the horse to move purely sideways, are illogical.[26]

DESCENT OF THE HAND AND OF THE LEG: A horse should maintain the position given him by his rider until asked to change it. When moving, his impulsion should continue without change until the rider asks for an increase or decrease. In the [wide] open, the well-trained horse maintains at all gaits the speed at which he is set just as a locomotive with a set throttle.

It is often said that a horse is off the hand when he stretches and lowers his head and neck to rid himself of the rider's hand or of the bridle which worries him. The correct meaning of the phrase is quite the opposite. The horse can be put off the hands when he is sufficiently trained *to fade off the reins, now mere threads which guide and support him.* The phrase "off the hands and legs" means simply that the horse receives no impression from them. In a word, the horse is completely free as long as he maintains the *position*, *gait*, and *speed* at which he has been set [by the rider]. The idea is to induce the horse to continue of his own accord without variation of the gait or to the movement that was commenced. The ability and willingness to go on his own is proof that the horse is truly balanced.

To teach the horse to go on his own, we begin by easing the hand slightly; if he displaces his head or stretches his neck, he is made to feel the bit. Continuing thus, he will gradually come to holding his position longer and longer, while we give him more and more freedom, and encourage him in this freedom. Similarly, he is taught to go without the action of the rider's legs.

---

26   [Beudant is not in favor of two track movements in general, hence his dislike of the diagonal effects used in their pure form, without any forward component.—*Editor's note*]

Outdoors, even more than in a school, we must leave the horse ALONE—on his own—and let his instinct come into play, for this serves him infinitely better than he could be served by even the most skilled rider. If, in crossing a swift stream, the horse hurts himself on a stone, steps into a hole or is carried downstream by the current, let the rider take good care not to pull on the reins, and the horse will probably carry him, safe and sound, to the other side. When, on a dangerous mountain trail, the horse must scramble up a steep slope or slide down a perpendicular bank, and the rider is sure there must be a fall, let him take courage, maintain his *aplomb* physically and mentally, let the horse have his head and go on his own. It is nearly certain that all will be well.

Outdoors, as in the *haute école,* a horse goes well only when he is balanced, and his balance is constantly changing to meet the demands of the moment. The maintenance of balance is the secret of a good riding horse. This is not to say that at fast gaits a horse should be thrown away. Contact with his mouth should be constant, and although it is sometimes reduced to the mere weight of the reins, he must have firmer support when at speed. It is the hand's ACTION on the mouth that ceases in certain cases, not its RELATIONSHIP with the horse's mouth. This RELATIONSHIP is always indispensable to both rider and horse; it gives confidence to the rider and enables him to direct his mount or to take him back smoothly as occasion requires.

Lightness

Lightness is the hall-mark of skillful riding, of advanced equitation, and stamps the rider who practices it as an expert. For the rider, it consists of having the horse light and easy to the legs as well as to the hands, or, as General L'Hotte put it:

> "To have the horse always smoothly flowing between the legs yet unseizable by them unless the hand opposes the forward movement."

Lightness to the Hands: The essentials for the rider are to be able to GUIDE, to HOLD, and to STOP his horse. Therefore the first thing to do in training a horse is to try from the very beginning to gradually obtain lightness by flexions of the jaw, done on foot if necessary. These flexions are especially important if the horse's mouth has been spoiled [by past riding experiences].

To make and maintain the horse's mouth must be the trainer's constant goal, regardless of the service for which the horse is intended. The pleasure horse is not pleasant unless his mouth is light, and a race horse with a bad mouth is difficult to handle. A "star-gazing" horse puts his nose in the air and avoids the bit instead of being on it, on account of a spoiled mouth, nor can he be made to stay on the bit by the rider's legs.

Lightness to the hands is that quality in a horse who obeys the reins without boring or hanging on the hands, or without the hands receiving any sensation of weight or tension more or less difficult to manage, or feeling any force that resists their action.

Lightness is recognized by the complete absence of any and all resistance to the effects of either or both bits. The merest tension on one or both reins should provoke mobility of the lower jaw without any derangement of the head; without more than the slightest opening of the mouth, the horse gently tonguing the bits. This soft mobility should last for an appreciable time and not stop abruptly.

True lightness is the infallible and never failing sign of balance. It is obtained by light, slow, soft tractions on the reins. Lightness, as just described, once obtained, the rider must be quick to ease his hands.

> "The horse is in exact balance, ready to submit to any action, and to take the position required for any movement that may be asked of him." (General Faverot de Kerbrech)

Hands: To produce lightness, FIXED hands, never approaching the rider's body, slowly squeezing adjusted reins, should make the lower jaw yield. If this lingering force does not supple and make the lower jaw mobile, then we must resort to vibrations to oppose the fixity of the lower jaw, and to half-halts to oppose the weight willfully and resistingly thrust forward.

VIBRATION: A shaking of one of the bits, either directly on foot or through the medium of a rein [either on foot or from the saddle (through the rein)].

HALF-HALT: An action by which the hand or hands move quickly without losing contact with the horse's mouth, and with a force much weaker than the resistance it attempts to overcome. This continuous contact with the mouth very clearly differentiates the half-halt from jerking [*saccade*]. The latter is brutal and useless and must never be used.[27]

FLEXIONS OF THE JAW:
    1.   *With the curb reins:* The trainer, on the [standing on foot to the] horse's left and a little to the rear of his head, holds the right curb rein in his right hand about six inches from the bit, and the left rein in his left hand about four inches from the bit; the horse's head is raised as high as possible and then the trainer brings his right hand quietly and lightly toward his body, and carries the left hand forward. If this action, continued for a few seconds, does not produce lightness, recourse must be had to the half-halt or vibrations, according to circumstances, using the left hand only. When the jaw becomes softly mobile, the hands are eased. Then the trainer moves to the right side and obtains similar flexions by similar means.
    2.   *With the snaffle reins:* The trainer places himself on the horse's left side as described for the

---

27   *Action par laquelle la main passe rapidement et sans cesser le contact avec la bouche, d'une force insuffisante à une force beaucoup plus grande. Le contact continuel avec la bouche différencie absolument le demi-arrêt de la saccade, procédé dangereux et dont l'usage doit être exclus du dressage du cheval de selle.* [For the sake of clarity the French has been included and the English revised. Editor's note.]

curb flexions, and raises the horse's head; holding the snaffle reins, crossed under the horse's neck, about six inches from the bit, the left rein in right hand, right rein in left, he obtains lightness by an equal, gradual, progressive and simultaneous traction on the two reins. When the jaw yields the hands are eased.

3. *With snaffle and curb rein on same side:* The trainer, on the left side, holding left snaffle rein in left hand and left curb rein in right, each at about six inches from the bit, raises the horse's head, and induces mobility of the lower jaw by carrying the left hand upward and forward, and right hand to rear, toward the horse's left shoulder. If the horse resists, use half-halt or vibrations on snaffle rein; when the lower jaw yields, the hands relax. This flexion is similarly repeated on the right side.

In the flexions, each time the horse yields he must be rewarded by a rest for a minute or two, with no tension whatsoever on the reins. The horse is thus gradually habituated to maintain the correct position himself. The flexions should be varied, sometimes using the rings of the snaffle or the branches of the curb instead of the reins. The training of a horse depends largely upon the way the flexions are done. It is very difficult to remake one that has been taught incorrect flexions.

Frequently, a trainer practicing the flexions eases his hands and rewards the horse when the horse abruptly brings his head to the vertical to avoid the pain of the bit on his bars; he opens his mouth and more or less relaxes his lower jaw. This is an incorrect and pernicious execution of the flexion. A horse with his neck thus abortively bent generally brings his head to the vertical or beyond, opens his mouth wide to avoid the bits, and thus completely escape all action of the hand. Flexions are directed at the lower JAW, not at the HEAD, which should remain as placed, high and immobile. In a correct flexion, the horse's tongue plays with the bits; his mouth opens softly and only a little; there is no stiffness; his head does not move during the flexion or for an appreciable time thereafter. In other words the horse merely smiles—he may even not open his mouth at all.

THE MOUTH: Is the same in all horses, and its resistance to the hand is due solely to the stiffness of the lower jaw, not to the sensitivity or insensitivity of the bars. In fact, there are more so called hard mouths among well-bred horses than among cold blooded ones.

An expert hand holds with a thread a horse that a much stronger but less skilled rider cannot manage at all. This fact proves that all mouths are the same. Obviously an expert rider cannot instantaneously change the horse's mouth!

It takes a long and varied experience to know a horse's mouth; to appreciate its delicate sensibilities when gently manipulated in contrast with its extreme resistance when force is roughly attempted. The horse that pulls our arms off can be managed with a single finger.

Neither the mouth nor the sides of a horse are naturally sensitive. In fact they are almost always cold to the bit and the heels. It is education to bit and spur that renders the mouth sensitive to almost imperceptible fingering of the reins, and the sides to mobilize to the slightest touch of the legs.

BITTING: It is a widespread belief that a horse requiring a snaffle only has a tender mouth and that the one requiring a curb is hard mouthed. Exactly the opposite is true. The snaffle is softer, it pains the horse less than the curb, only when used as a halter merely to guide the horse. When the snaffle is substituted for the curb it is more severe than the latter. I grant that in expert hands the snaffle readily destroys all resistance, but generally the mouth made with the curb is ready for the snaffle, while a lower jaw that gives to the snaffle often resists the curb unless specially prepared for it. The reason for the soft mouths of horses ridden by Arabs is that their horses are always ridden with the curb bit [first]. It is the exception when one sees an Arab's horse boring on the bit. In training it is more practical to begin with the curb and only later to change to the snaffle.

International Horse Show at Nice.
Captain De Lassardière and Major Horment (France) on Grey Fox and Psyche respectively.

ACTION OF THE HANDS: An old rusty lock is stubborn and difficult to open. After many fruitless attempts we are likely to grow impatient and try to force it. We waste our time and energy, and end up twisting or breaking the key with the lock still unopened. Suppose, on the contrary, we send for a locksmith; he gently takes the key and with no effort—presto!—the lock clicks open. Here we have the action of the hands.

There is an astonishing relationship between a horse's mouth and the muscles throughout his body. In resisting his rider, a horse cannot contract a single muscle without simultaneously contracting his lower jaw. Conversely, the lighter his mouth, the better his balance is.

For example, take an unsuppled horse that stiffens and breaks up at the gallop. Regardless of how good a galloper he may be, the gait becomes broken, irregular, and distorted the moment he feels a jerk on the mouth or any other *faux pas* of heavy, hard hands. On the contrary, if hands are light and easy, his mouth remains soft; his gallop continues regular and rhythmic; the rider feels no disagreeable reaction—proof that the mouth is a flawless indicator of body suppleness—proof also that the least action on his mouth results in reaction in the horse's entire body.

Once lightness of the mouth is obtained, resistance disappears regardless of the location. The horse becomes balanced, or said another way, resumes his natural balance.

The essential result is that good execution of balance in the movement demands that lightness remains. This demonstrates conclusively that obtaining, then maintaining lightness, must be the constant preoccupation of the rider.

GOOD HANDS: Like the phrases descriptive of a horse's mouth, expressions about the rider's hands are usually misleading and inexact. "Jones' hands are hard." "This horse has a hard mouth." "Tom has light hands." "The bay mare is soft-mouthed." These and similar expressions do not mean what they say. With reference to their hands there are only two classes of riders: The horseman who can, and the one who cannot give to his hands, whether they are strong or feeble, that FIXITY which, when outdoors, enables him to hold the pulling horse, and which in the school, in the most difficult airs and moments of the *haute école,* permits him to act upon the horse's mouth without the slightest hindrance to the prodigious impulsion required.

LIGHTNESS OF THE HAUNCHES: *Petites attaques.* If the horse is cold to the heel, we must resort to *petites attaques.* In other words, when the calves of the legs fail to produce the desired effect, the spur comes immediately to reinforce them. In the *petites attaques* the spur pricks quickly; it never remains in or on the horse for an appreciable time. It is like the prick of the surgeon's lancet in blood-letting. The mere contact[28] of the boot should be sufficient to obtain or to increase impulsion, or to displace the haunches. This extreme delicacy of the haunches means their perfect obedience; it does not mean fear of the legs or an irritable sensitiveness. The well-trained horse fears neither hand nor leg nor spur. He is not difficult to mount, and is not upset by the contact of the heel. He accepts the aids without disturbance but obeys their slightest indication. Comte d'Aure's simile on page 27 gives the picture of impulsion, indispensable for outdoor riding as well as for *haute école*. Life and brilliancy come only from impulsion.

From the exercises which follow, one should select those best suited to the intended purpose.

The schedule of training is merely a summary, with some explanatory remarks of the teachings of General Faverot de Kerbrech whose ideas I have faithfully tried to interpret.

To avoid confusion, the work is supposed to be done in a rectangular enclosure.

The word "lightness" will mean that the rider has contact with the horse's mouth; that the lower jaw is relaxed or softly mobile, depending upon whether it is a case of ordinary or of higher training. The trainer should understand that the horse must be light at all times—for each and every movement, although I have used the word "lightness" only occasionally.

---

28   Some French horseman has poetically and aptly described this delicate finesse in saying of a well-trained sensitive horse: *"Il travaille au vents des bottes."*—"He works on the wind of the boot." —*Translator's note.*

Progression of Dressage

TO MOUNT WITH THE HELP OF AN ASSISTANT: The rider on the near side strokes and pets the horse; if the horse moves, the assistant immediately stops him. The rider takes hold of the mane; snaps the stirrup leather against saddle skirt, puts his foot in the stirrup, then removes it; repeats this, and finally seats himself into the saddle. Repeat the same routine on the off side.

TO MOVE THE HORSE FORWARD: Lightness; close the legs, lower the hands, and as soon as the horse moves forward relax the legs.

TO HALT: Raise the hands with tension on the reins; legs are not closed but are ready to steady the horse or to prevent him from backing.

TO REIN-BACK: Lightness; raise the hands with tension on the reins; no legs. Once the horse backs, try to make him understand that he is to back without indication from the rein. Use legs to stop him [backing] or to move him to the front.

TO TURN: First: By the inside rein (direct rein): carry the hand outward without increasing tension on the rein.
Second: By the outside rein (indirect rein): raise the hands and carry them to the right (or left) without increasing tension on the reins.

TO SIDE STEP: The head, then the croup to the wall. The inside (side towards which the horse is to move) leg acts first and prepares the horse for the movement; then the outside leg pushes him a step or two; stop; obtain lightness; reward him; repeat. Repeat the same work to other hand.

PIROUETTES: One step, stop, obtain lightness, [repeat] etc., etc. In the pirouette on the haunches, only the outside leg acts. In the pirouette on the forehand, the outside rein is substituted for the outside leg to the greatest possible extent.

Circles, Half-Circles, Diagonal Change of Hand: In these exercises hold the haunches. First demand one step, then two, three, and so on.

Obedience to the Spur

The horse, having acquired the habit of general obedience, must then be familiarized with the spur.

Ordinary Training: To teach the horse to go forward at the touch of the spur: lower the hands; apply the spur very quietly and gradually; the moment the horse moves forward the spur's action ceases. If, as sometimes happens, the horse backs instead of moving to the front, attack him boldly and vigorously with the spurs, or even use the whip until he moves forward. Reward him as soon as he obeys. If he kicks at the spur, use half-halts more or less energetically, and if necessary hit him with the whip at the moment of the kick.

Advanced Training: A horse must obey the spur as the dutiful son obeys his father—completely and unhesitatingly; quietly, but quickly if need be; never brusquely or with bad humor. To instill this obedience in the horse, the rider must act with an inflexible but calm authority. General Faverot de Kerbrech on this subject says:

> "The rider first places his legs against the horse, then demands lightness; now he closes his legs quietly and gradually with increasing pressure. If the horse moves forward, stop him with the snaffle. If he remains calm and light while the legs close with considerable pressure, be quick to ease off and reward the horse. If he moves or is restless, continue the leg pressure without increasing it, and apply half-halts until immobility is reestablished; then immediately relax the legs and reward the horse. The next steps are: to teach him to bear the heels, the dummy spurs, and lastly the rowels."

Generally the dummy spurs may be omitted.

International Horse Show at Nice. Major Cafaretti on Fenomeno.

TO MARCH ON THE SPUR: When the horse at the halt bears the spurs, he must be taught to bear them while moving. Proceed as follows: let the spurs rest in the hair of the horse's sides while he is light and immobile due to the action of the hands; lower the hands slightly, and quietly increase the pressure of the spurs. When the horse moves forward, immediately relax the legs and then cease the action with the hands. This lesson is repeated until the horse is confirmed in marching on the spur.

SUPPORT OF THE SPUR AT THE WALK: The action of the spur is frank but quiet; hands prevent an increase of gait. Be careful to avoid a weak, timid application of the spur, which merely tickles and irritates the horse. If the spurs resting in the hair upset the horse, calm him and reestablish regularity of gait. It may be necessary to revert back to the lesson in place.

From the Walk to the Trot on the Spur: When the horse is confirmed at the walk on the spur, he must be taught to accept it at the collected trot; the hands should prevent increase of speed. Finally proceed from the halt to the walk, to the collected trot, to the regular trot, in the same way as was done from the halt to the walk. The horse now knows the spur, and he is certain to have impulsion when needed because he has learned to go always to the front at the call of the spurs.

Effet d'ensemble on the spur[29]

This is not within reach of all who ride: it is like a razor in the hands of a monkey.

I will give a summary of the way General Faverot de Kerbrech recommends it be practiced.

The first requisite of success is to prevent the horse from stretching his neck and sticking out his nose. The reins, therefore, must be short, and the curb rein is usually surer than the snaffle. At any rate, the rider must not give in; he must prevent the horse from stretching his head and neck.

The legs close gradually, simultaneously, and forcefully until a frank support of the spurs is reached; the hands continue opposition until this vigorous, gradual, and simultaneous action of legs and spurs, pushing the mass against the restraining bit, produces immobility; or if the horse is moving, regularity of gait. As soon as the horse becomes light, the hands, and then the spurs, and lastly the legs ease off. The *effet d'ensemble* frankly practiced is the only absolute way of preventing every defense. Even after the horse has been confirmed in its practice, a part of each training period must be devoted to this lesson.

If the horse backs at the touch of the spurs, he must be vigorously attacked until he moves forward. This defense of backing is not likely to occur if the progressive steps indicated have been carefully followed. A horse must always go into the bit at the call of the spur; the more vigorous the call, the freer the

---

29   Obedience to the spur

response. Even when the *effet d'ensemble* is practiced in place he must go into the bit at the touch of the spurs. In this case he does not advance; the forward movement finishes at the bits which makes the lower jaw yield.

If the horse kicks at the touch of the spur, punish him with a cut of the whip just behind the boot: cut him only once, but give him a good one and at the moment of the kick.

It must be thoroughly understood that the action of the spur is not at one time to immobilize the horse, and at another time to carry him forward. Its action is *always to carry him to the front;* always to *exact propulsion* which the hand alone diminishes or destroys. Its action must be graduated to the temperament of the horse, to the sensitiveness of his sides. Obviously it would be foolish to use spurs harshly on a highly sensitive horse and then have to palliate this brutality by bit-action such as a teamster [driver] employs with a mule.

The *effet d'ensemble* produces results and is of universal application, regardless of the horse's temperament or disposition which of course varies by the individual.

> "However vicious he may be, the animal quickly learns that resistance is in vain. This feeling of helplessness causes him to abandon the struggle; his spirit is subdued; he is resigned to obedience." (General Faverot de Kerbrech)

The horse that is habituated to the *effet d'ensemble* never dreams of disobeying a rider who can employ it; its utility in ordinary equitation is indisputable; it is exactly what is needed: the horse can be compelled to go to the front under any and all conditions. The steeplechaser should be so inured to it that his rider can prevent a run-out and be master under all conditions.

Accord of the Aids

The hands must never impair the force which produces the movement. The force which pushes the mass must carry along only that small proportion of weight that the movement entails. In training, of all the faults of the hand the most general and the worst is the hand's impairment of impulsion.

The *Ramener*

The *ramener* brings the horse's face almost to the vertical. First, the jaw must yield, the head remaining high and immobile; then having obtained lightness, the head by a bend at the poll assumes the vertical or nearly vertical position; its exact position depends upon how it is attached [conformationally] to the neck.

The hands act alone—without legs, without impairing movement, without slowing the gait—on a single rein, or by alternate or combined action of [curb] bit and bridoon, as the individual case may require. It is not the POSITION of the head that causes lightness; it is the MOBILITY of the lower jaw [that produces lightness]. Lightness is the cause; position the effect. Therefore, seek the cause exclusively; the effect will follow. When the hand, through the medium of a powerful bit, pulls the head to the vertical, and forces the mouth to open, the BALANCE known as LIGHTNESS is never obtained; the horse is always resisting—a condition completely absent in lightness.

The forced compression of the head and lower jaw, under the influence of a cruel bit and powerful legs, does not imply the relaxation of the muscles of those parts, and still less the yielding of the muscles of the rest of the body. True, the position has been attained, but actually, [in this case] contraction has been increased. On the contrary, when the hand with its delicate INSINUATIONS induces the relaxation of the muscles of the jaw, all other muscles relax because the horse, inspired with confidence, entrusts himself to his rider. Rid of the irksome force which caused him to contract and stiffen, he returns to true balance manifested by lightness of the mouth. To try to supple a horse at the trot or gallop is to attempt a task often impossible. It is in place or at the walk, and nowhere else, that one can quickly make the horse light from mouth to haunches; such that all resistance can be obliterated.

AT THE TROT: Repeat at the slow trot the work done at the walk. Do not be in a hurry; do not attempt the *ramener* at the slow trot until it has been perfected at the walk; until the horse is light; his neck high, his head in position. In all cases, whatever the gait, the horse when light must be allowed the greatest possible freedom. "When he thinks he is our master, then he is our slave." (Baucher) However, he must never be allowed to do what was not asked of him.

The *Rassembler*

The *rassembler* consists of provoking, without perceptible advancement, the play, the functioning of all muscles to obtain "action in place," or if the horse is moving, to augment his action without appreciably increasing his speed. "It is only through the *rassembler* that a horse can be put in exact balance; that the length of his base of support and the height of his action can be regulated exactly as the rider requires." (General Faverot de Kerbrech)

The *rassembler* means not at all what it is generally supposed to mean. Ordinarily a horse in place is considered *en rassembler* when, with base of support shortened by bringing his fore and hind feet closer together through action of rider's hands and legs, he stands IMMOBILE and in a balance easy to break in ONE direction only—that of the anticipated movement.

In the true *rassembler* in place, the horse is clearly and distinctly in a balance easy to break in ANY direction, and he is in ACTION. The true *rassembler* is not only a concentration of weight, but also a concentration of energy.

To obtain the *rassembler* in place, have the horse straight and light; animate him by light taps of the legs reinforced if necessary by the spurs; receive on the hands the action produced by the legs and spurs; and it will he projected upward instead of escaping in forward movement. This action, at first, is only a suspicion of mobility; later, the hind legs advance almost imperceptibly to get nearer to the center of gravity; there is movement of the forelegs, but they gain ground neither to front nor rear. The *rassembler* in place leads naturally to the *piaffer*. Great tact is required. Proceed slowly; reward the least effort towards obedience; if the horse gets out of alignment, straighten him; insist on lightness; never demand mobility of his supports [legs] except when the horse is light[30].

DIFFERENCE BETWEEN EFFET D'ENSEMBLE AND RASSEMBLER:
The former calms, appeases or rules; hands and legs act *simultaneously,* progressively, continuously; whereas the *rassembler* animates, awakes, excites activity; gives life and brilliance; hands and legs act *alternately.*

Work at the Canter

CANTER-DEPARTS:
   First: being at the walk, place the horse's head with the direct rein and act in the same way as to depart at the trot. The horse will take the lead for which he is set.
   Second: being at the walk on a circle, set the horse with the inside rein; use both legs, use the inside leg first. Action operating on position produces the gallop on the inside lead.
   Third: if a horse has the habit of cantering traversed—with his haunches out of alignment[to the inside]—put him into the canter by means of an inside indirect rein; the tension on this [inside] rein should be from below, upwards; reinforce the [inside] rein with equal pressure of both legs. Before trying to put him into the canter, have him absolutely straight—with his haunches directly behind his shoulders.
   When one wishes to go further in training, the surest

---

30   Baucher compares the horse in perfect *rassembler* to a set of balances which the rider, by the slightest movement, can tip in any direction; he adds that the rider will know when the *rassembler* is complete, for he will feel that the horse is ready to leave the earth. *Translator's note.*

Captain McMahon, U. S. A. *Aplomb!*

and quickest way of obtaining a canter-depart is as follows: never think of a canter-depart until the horse knows the *piaffer*. Then, and only then, demand the depart by setting the horse's head and raising it with a snaffle rein, legs passive. By this method two-track work, changes of lead at the canter, etc., are easily taught, because the *piaffer well-done is the key to the complete possession of the horse's forces.*

The canter should be very regular, smooth, and rhythmic. Often switch from one set of reins to the other. If the horse tries to increase the speed, calm him. Practice counter canter [false] departs; true and false canter departs on a circle. Keep the horse straight; if he shifts his haunches to one side, use an indirect rein to straighten him. Give him much work on his own, properly balanced—no hands, no legs. Practice backing; work on small circles.

CANTER ON TWO TRACKS: Demand a few steps only; reward; come back to walk; repeat.

DIAGONAL CHANGE OF HAND: Two or three steps, holding the haunches; come to walk (action of inside leg). When horse is well-trained the hands are the main aids.

Circles at the Canter on Two Tracks: Half Turns at the Canter on Two Tracks, Half-Turns in Reverse, Pirouettes at the Canter: Describe small figures; commence each figure at a walk; end it at a canter.

Circles at the Canter on Two Tracks: Commence at the walk, then one or two strides at the gallop; gradually increase the number of gallop strides.

Canter-Depart by Hand-Aids Only: This may be obtained in one of the two ways, with the horse always remaining straight:

First: To Depart on Right Lead by Right Direct Rein. Starting at the walk, rouse the horse without decreasing speed, by a slight half-halt on right rein, executed while carrying right hand upward and to left; if he slows, ease hands; use legs, especially the right leg, to push him to the front; try again for the depart.

Second: To Depart on Right Lead by Right Indirect Rein: Starting at the walk, with the horse light; lower the right hand to left, then raise and carry it to the right, at the same time pushing the neck with the left rein. If the horse slows, ease the hands; use the legs to reestablish impulsion, and then again attempt the depart. This is rocking the horse, a procedure in which the rider rocks or rolls him with each stride to give him life and animation. By these means the horse quickly learns to depart at the canter straight and almost at the thought of the rider, transmitted of course through the reins. This method of taking the canter is particularly useful out-of-doors.

Canter on Two Tracks by Hand-Aids Only: Before attempting the two tracks, put the horse at the collected canter by means of half-halts; no legs. If his action decreases ease the hands, and use the legs to reestablish impulsion.

Canter-Depart with Leg-Aids Only: Starting at the walk, drop reins on horse's neck. If he trots at the pressure of the legs, relax them entirely; stop him by half-halts. The walk being resumed, again try the canter-depart by leg-aids only.

CHANGE OF LEAD AT THE GALLOP: By means of the reins, set the horse's head as for a canter-depart—let the horse do the rest. If he slows, use legs or spurs if necessary to reestablish impulsion. While impulsion is being reestablished, do not act with the hands and do not attempt the change of lead. When impulsion is again sufficient, reset the head; if impulsion again dies, abandon the set, and reestablish impulsion by use of legs, no hands; then again set the head. Remember that the change of leg is from the position; leg-aids play little or no part in the change. The horse will change when his impulsion is sufficient. He should not increase speed; if he does, stop short, calm him, begin again. For this work be careful to use hands without legs; leg-aids are used very little, if at all. The horse himself should change. Never upset or excite him. With an animal of sufficient action, never use the legs to prevent him changing behind before he changes in front. When the horse lacks impulsion to such an extent that setting his head leaves him insufficient action to effect the change, the rider's legs should act first; then the set is immediately given.

CHANGE OF LEAD BY LEG-AIDS ONLY: Reins on horse's neck; use both legs, especially the one on the side to which the change is demanded.

REPEATED CHANGES OF LEAD: [SEQUENCE OR TEMPI CHANGES]
That is, changes from right to left and from left to right with only a few strides intervening. If there is sufficient impulsion, the easiest method is by hand-aids only. Gradually bring the changes closer and closer together. Do not hurry the horse; give him the position; let him do the changing. The displacements of rider's hand must be accurate and distinct; intelligible to the horse.

Before repeated changes of lead can be made by the leg-aids only, the horse must be so well disciplined that with the reins on his neck he makes no attempt to increase the speed when the rider's legs are applied. A sudden increase of speed is likely to mean loss of balance. If a change is to be made from left to right, for example, the rider's left leg indicates the maneuver, but his right leg determines it.

The number of strides between changes is gradually decreased, until finally the horse is asked to change at every other stride, and then at every stride. Until the horse has become confirmed in rapid, repeated changes, always rest and reward him

International Horse Show at Nice
Pair Jumping, Commandant Horment and Lt. La Maissonneuve.

after a pair of changes [a series of two successful sequence changes when he is learning them].

For these lessons the horse must be absolutely calm; if he becomes excited, increases his speed, or alters his balance, do not attempt the change. Stop, calm him then start anew.

The rider should guard against displacing his seat—shifting his weight. The hands—or if change is demanded by legs—the legs only act softly and smoothly. Most important of all, beware of jerks or roughness in any form! The horse must have sufficient action; if action is lacking, or if hands impede impulsion, the hind legs cannot change with the fore[31]. Always remember that in a true change of lead the change is made in the air, during the period of suspension.

---

31   Editor's note: The author is referring to the fact that if the hand restricts or arrests the forehand, the horse will not be able to 'jump through' and change together simultaneously. Likewise, if the hand blocks or inhibits the action or impulsion of the haunches there will not be enough 'jump' to change over to the new lead. Therefore, the feeling of the hands, and the impact that they have on the straightness, balance, alignment, collection, roundness, activity of the haunches, and freedom of the front legs is critical to the success of the flying changes.

The change of lead at each stride is difficult, and Fillis has aptly said: "The horseman who obtains a correct change of lead at every stride on a circle may well be satisfied with himself and his horse."

"To succeed, avoid asking a horse for this difficult task when he is tired, unstrung, or wet with sweat; under these conditions the change must be obtained by force. For a difficult lesson, the animal should be fresh; then the lesson is sport intermixed with rewards and rests." (General Faverot de Kerbrech)

The horse learns his part readily enough; not so the man; to him, only after long practice comes the cunning skill to act with hand or leg at the fleeting moment when to act is to succeed.

THE EXTENDED CANTER: Confirm the horse in maintaining uniform speeds as the canter is progressively accelerated. As the speed increases mobility of the jaw decreases.

TO HALT FROM FAST CANTER: Use the hands, strongly if need be, until horse halts; at the moment of halting lower the hands to permit that stretching of the neck so essential to the role of the hocks in halting. Back him immediately after halting.

The Grand Trot

Take the collected trot, and when it has become very regular gradually lengthen it. If the grand trot is not lively and bold, or if lightness is lost, stop short; obtain lightness; relax; begin again. Practice this with descents of the hand.

Jumping

First develop the horse's natural aptitude for jumping. On the longe and at liberty make him willing and bold. Proceed slowly and gradually, to avoid the possibility of getting him sour, discouraged, or apprehensive of the obstacle; be careful not to jump him when he is tired and thus risk provoking resistance. In jumping more than in any other phase of training the horse must develop a taste for the work; he must be interested, and ambitious to make each jump better than the preceding one.

For a good show-jumper, a hunter, or a steeple chaser seek above all else a horse full of energy. The sluggish fellow, regardless of his power, will never do. A horse can jump his best only when he is well muscled and in good general condition. Therefore he should be in condition, well muscled and in good wind before he is asked to take big jumps. The best method of conditioning a jumper is by much jumping at a walk and a trot over small obstacles.

He should not be ridden over jumps until his training has advanced to such a point that his rider is sure of being able to put him over any obstacle within the horse's ability. (*Effet d'ensemble* on the spur.)

The rider should be especially careful about his seat, which exerts an enormous influence on the horse's willingness and power over jumps.

No other single factor is so important throughout the horse's jumping career. The seat may be summed up as follows: preserve the greatest possible independence of all parts of the body. Independence of all parts of the body means, for example, that the closing of the thighs with all their strength does not cause the slightest contraction in the loins, which must always be supple; the closing of the thighs must in no way disturb the seat, which should remain quiet on the saddle.

Similarly, the rider should be able to close his knees and calves without touching the horse with heel or spur. At times, with fingers tightly clenching the reins, his hands and arms must follow the horse's head as though they were rubber bands extending from rider's shoulders to horse's mouth. When at speed, the rider inclines his body to the front and raises his seat from the saddle, the buttocks should be pushed forward, not "stuck out" behind in the air. In other words, the rider is seated but on knees and thighs only; his hands are fixed and always low. Often riders pretend to relieve the horse's loins by "sticking their posteriors out behind." Their form is the result of their inability to ride correctly rather than a reasoned attempt to help the horse. With good riders it is different.

Captain Lequio, one of Italy's best
demonstrating the Italian jumping seat at its perfection

It seems to me that here, as elsewhere, neither seat nor weight should be displaced. I thoroughly understand that in inclining his body to the front, the rider seeks greater speed or more power over the jump. Yet in jumping, as in the *haute école,* for instance, in the change of lead at the canter, I believe good execution requires that the horse be left alone; that he be left free to dispose of his forces, whether in handling the total mass (rider and horse), or in resisting the inertia of that mass. I believe it is extremely difficult for the rider to act with more *apropos* than can the horse, guided by his instinct for balance. For my part, I try to avoid affecting in the slightest degree the horse's balance by seat displacements which his instinct cannot possibly foresee. My advice to the rider is: let him maintain the same position over the jump that he had at the take-off, whether his seat is in the saddle or out of it.

Few riders have enough suppleness in their loins to remain comfortably seated in the saddle for long periods at a fast gallop, or over jumps. There are a few that are so supple, and so "with the horse," that thus seated they tire neither themselves nor their horses.

Courtesy of "The Sportsman"
International Horse Show at Rome
1930 the Most Difficult Show Ring in the World.
Captain Count Borsarelli, Italy, on Crispa clearing 15'-6" of water with a triple bar 4'-11", 7'-3" spread, Compare this picture with the one opposite. Here the rider is WITH HIS HORSE.

It is evident that a seat with the body inclined to the front, supported below by thighs, knees and stirrups—all reinforced by hands resting on either side of the withers—is very secure, and relieves the spinal columns of horse and rider of many jolts. Such a seat also relieves the horse's hindquarters and lends fixity, a security against sudden and inopportune derangement of weight. These considerations make the racing seat the most favorable to speed, also to power over the jumps.

Be that as it may, when it comes to jumping, the main factor in man or horse is *nerve*.

Often in our dreams we fly over enormous fences, but in hunting when we come to a solid fence no more than one meter high, our horse stops or runs out. Why? We do not have the will to jump—our hearts remain on the sidelines.

What I say, or what even the most accomplished cross-country riders might say, is little as compared to what practice or even observation teaches.

Courtesy of "The Sportsman." Left at the Post
The rider, though giving his horse plenty of head, is BEHIND. The horse, in addition to the enormous jump, has the inertia of the rider to contend with. To clear the jump this horse's effort must be far greater than his successful competitor opposite.

For their courtesy and kindness in permitting the use of photographs, I am very grateful to the Marquis of Maleissye, to Captain C. de Salverte, and to the entire committee of the International Horse Show at Nice.

These pictures make a most agreeable impression, and serve a most useful purpose. No theory or words could describe so well that bold *assurance* of rider which inspires his horse to incredible leaps; that wonderful *fixity of hand without which* no jump is well done regardless of the seat adopted.

An attentive examination of the attitude, bearing, and seat of these horsemen *d'elite,* and of their horses' heads, I am sure will be very profitable. A four foot fence and ten feet of water are serious obstacles; solid jumps up to five feet in height or thirteen feet in width must be left to intrepid riders astride courageous, well-trained, indomitable horses.

To merit the name horseman, one must subscribe to the words of the gallant Captain Bauzil, killed on the race course at Saint-Omer: "We must always be ready to gallop, to jump—yes, and to fall; only those who do not ride, do not fall; we will not break our necks until our time comes." (Paris-Rouen-Deauville)

Out-of-Doors [Outdoor Riding]

Outdoor work is the horse's sole *raison d'etre* [reason for being alive]. The training indicated thus far embraces only the supplings necessary to make him manageable and sure over country.

The more skillful the rider, the more he appreciates perfection in the training of the horse he rides. In other words, the abler and more experienced the rider, the further he carries the training and finesse of his horse. The training heretofore prescribed is not sufficient for a real charger—a true *cheval d'armes*.

Suppleness, lightness of the jaw and the haunches, elevation of the head and neck; all these help to make the horse more agreeable. Due to his suppleness he escapes, when mounted by a stiff and awkward rider, those baneful influences which provoke incorrect positions and loss of balance.

The well-trained horse, well-ridden, neither stiffens his neck nor through its excessive flexion brings his chin to his breast; he does not travel sideways. He uses his energy judiciously; he does not get leg-weary at the gallop, because he changes to the left lead when he tires of the right. Similarly, the good rider does not habitually post on one diagonal and thus overwork it; he opportunely changes diagonals. Finally, both horse and rider are spared the fatigue and discomfort of rough, irregular, stiff gaits.

But a good outdoor horse, a charger, can never be made by school work alone. A good riding horse should go on all sorts of roads with the reins on his neck; he must go over difficult places without stumbling or falling. By experience he must learn to choose his terrain and to watch where he puts his feet. When he wants to rush a bank or a ditch, the rider should simply use

Captain Bradford, U. S. A., on Buckaroo
Legs fixed, firm as a rock; hands steady but movable
following horse's head

the reins to prevent the increase of speed and do nothing else. In a short time the horse will lose his desire to rush accidents and irregularities of ground. Obstacles that do not require jumping, he should overcome without jumping—by stepping over them.

Outdoors the reins should be used as little as possible, and in using them the hands should not be displaced. The only effort of the rider should be to prevent a horse from boring on the bit or from throwing away his lower jaw while arching his neck in an extreme curve. The horse should be straight and horizontal at the walk, and a little elevated at the faster gaits. He should be held by the simple action of take and give—as though he were ridden in a halter.

By alternating outdoor training with school training, a real charger is developed—a horse that quickly understands the intent of his rider—whether he means high collection, simple direction, decrease of speed, halt or whatever. Such a horse approaches the ideal; at his master's will he collects himself and parades, or travels quietly in troop-column; he runs and jumps as a horse at liberty.

Haut École

The *haute école* is the quest for complete possession of the forces of the horse so that the rider may dispose of them as he wills—may play upon them as he wishes.

From this definition comes the formula that lightness is the base of higher equitation.

In this equitation of fantasy, faults nearly always, if not always, come from lack of impulsion.

On the other hand, no air is well done if the mouth is not light, because this lightness is the index of balance.

Many officers are openly hostile to the *haute école*. They reason thus:

> 1st. The high schooled horse is generally too much for a trooper.
> 2nd. He frequently takes these artificial gaits in spite of his rider, thereby needlessly tiring both himself and rider, and in addition throwing the ranks into disorder.
> 3rd. The *haute école* captivates its devotees and tends to alienate them from the true goal of military horsemen—boldness, skill, and endurance in the open.
> 4th. A man may resort to violence in trying to teach his horses the airs of the school and thus spoil their dispositions and otherwise injure them.

According to them, the *haute école* and equitation of fantasy is only a luxury—an elegant veneer. On the contrary, the airs of the *haute école,* the gymnastics of its artificial gaits, while entirely unnecessary for ordinary training, are the best means by which to arrive at the perfection of that training.[32]

The basic work of the *haute école* is the *piaffer* which becomes the *passage* when executed while advancing. The *piaffer* demands an extreme concentration of forces and, as jumping, is one of the best exercises to strengthen and develop the hindquarters. Likewise, the Spanish trot is the way *par excellence* to develop

---

32   Gustave le Bon, the French psychologist, who studied riding and horses, says that the *haute école* is the base, not the crown, of intelligent riding.—*Translator's note.*

the mobility of the shoulders. Thus from these two exercises we produce a balanced horse; one with extreme mobility and play of the shoulders, propelled by strong and muscular hindquarters—certainly two highly desirable conditions in a riding horse.

The *haute école* and equitation of fantasy are at once both a refinement *de luxe* and a practical means of arriving at perfection.

Before attempting high school training, we should be sure that our horse is absolutely confirmed in the requirements of ordinary training. We must be sure that we will not spoil a good horse by asking too much of him before he is ready. Finally we must never try to high school a horse until he is so disciplined that we are certain of our ability to prevent him from taking of his own accord, as a defense, the airs we teach him.

The airs of fantasy may be taught by either of two distinctly different methods:

1st. By equitation, properly called, which operates through the medium of the aids.
2nd. By circus-training, which makes no pretense at using the natural aids.

A combination of these two methods is attempted by some charlatans, but the result cannot be called higher equitation. In this circus-training, the horse learns by heart some movements and airs of the *haute école* which he always repeats in exactly the same order. He is merely routined.[33]

The training of the true *haute école* is totally different. It produces a light horse; it destroys all contractions which oppose complete obedience of the various parts of the horse's body to the rider's aids. The horse thus trained is not routined; he repeats nothing by heart; he varies and modifies the airs at the inspiration of the artist astride him.

This training, statements to the contrary notwithstanding, is applicable to all riding horses, regardless of conformation.

I have many times repeated that the *great stumbling block* of training is the *folly of mistaking effects for causes—the folly of*

---

33   The real masters of the *haute école* call this "poodle dog training."—*Translator's note.*

attacking effects instead of destroying their causes. This is especially true in the *haute école*. There, as in all other delicate situations, the key to success is lightness. Without lightness it is difficult if not impossible to execute any but the simplest movements; with it, nothing is difficult.

> "At its perfection, the merest *nuance* of the aids brings into play all the muscles that incite impulsion, and thereby obtains correct distribution of the forces so necessary to the complete harmony of the movement." (General L'Hotte)

When a horse is light he is a perfectly tuned keyboard upon which the artist plays the most harmonious airs.

De Lubersac trained his horses at the walk only, and when he had finished, they were perfectly trained for all gaits.

General L'Hotte said: "His infinite tact enabled him to feel at the walk all resistance, however slight, and with his marvellous skill he destroyed it at its very roots." Training which produces such perfection is the true *haute école;* in addition, it includes the airs and gaits of fantasy.

Work, experience, and scientific theories are of value in this transcendent and artistic equitation, but pre-eminence comes only to him who has a passion for the art.

The masterpieces in equitation are not realized as might be inferred from the often heard exclamation, "What patience he must have!" These *chefs-d'oeuvre* are all the more difficult when the artist must rely upon imagination without skilled fingers to help, or upon sensitive fingers unguided by the airy goddess of fancy. The horseman does not play upon musical chords that always give the same tone to the same touch; he must vibrate live muscle influenced by caprice and energy and ardor. To aid his imagination, the artist on horseback has to coordinate, at a moment precise and fleeting, his thoughts, his will, his muscles with the will and muscles of the horse.

General Faverot de Kerbrech said: "With the *piaffer*, we enter the realm of the equitation of fantasy, scholarly riding, full of thrills and joys; essential, if we aim at perfection, but not indispensable for regular training."

Lt. Wofford, U.S.A., in a Good Landing
The seat is returning to the saddle. The rider landed on his stirrups, calves, knees, and lower thighs; his weight was suspended; his relaxed ankles, low heels, bent and relaxed knees, and relaxed hip joints all acted as shock absorbers. The horse's back was relieved of a tremendous blow.

The domain of this equitation is limitless. It begins where ordinary riding ends—after the natural gaits and movements have been perfected *(passage,* extended trot, change of lead at the canter, etc.). It comprises airs and gaits which the horse at liberty never uses (two tracks, *piaffer,* Spanish trot, trot-to-the-rear and gallop-to-the-rear, gallop on three legs, etc.). Finally, it includes movements contrary to the simple laws of mechanics (Robersart II, Iris, Mimoun; canter on two tracks to the non-lead side [leg-yield in the canter or *plié-gallop*], pirouettes and reversed pirouettes at the counter-canter).

The most brilliant airs are not necessarily the most valuable for training. The talent of the horseman must be judged by his horses; by the perfection and accuracy of their execution in response to the aids. The work at the canter, the changes of gait, especially modifications in the extension and cadence of gaits—

Lt.-Col. Merchant, U. S. A., on Jack Snipe
There is less thrust off a bank than over an obstacle; therefore the seat remains closer to the saddle in the former case than in the latter.

these are the criteria of the *haute école.* A horse may do the *piaffer,* the *passage,* the Spanish trot, and still he ignorant of the aids. But to change from one of these gaits to another in response to the aids; from the right two track to the left, from the pirouette to the pirouette reversed, etc.—such immediate and exact obedience to the aids is really the *haute école,* whose best fruit is a horse light and balanced at all gaits and in all circumstances.

No pleasure to be had with horses is comparable to riding a perfectly trained one.

POSITION OF THE RIDER: At first thought it may seem that a system of training is not concerned with the POSITION of the rider; that POSITION properly belongs in the domain of equitation. Nevertheless, the way a rider sits on his horse is so intimately connected with the question of the horse's balance that a few words on position-in-the-saddle may not be out, of place.

Head high, knees low, or more or less raised, shoulders

rounded or square—these details matter little; the main tiling is *aplomb.* **Evidently, if the weight of the rider is to one side of the saddle, the much sought-after balance is not so easily obtained or maintained as when the rider is in the middle of the saddle.**

The position of the legs is of considerable importance. A stirrup too long renders leg action difficult because then the rider slides his legs to the front or swings his legs to avoid losing his stirrups. The legs should hang near the horse's sides.

It is frequently said of a rider whose thighs are well let down that he rides too long; of another who is "hunched up" that he rides too short. Neither of these expressions is accurate. The stirrup is short when, without moving his knee, the rider gets it with difficulty; it is long when the sole of the boot barely touches it—the rider is fishing for the stirrup. One may have stirrups short, and thighs well let down; and inversely, knees may be tucked up when stirrups are too long.

The cardinal requisite is to be SEATED; the rest is of little importance save the length of stirrup, which should be just right—neither too long nor too short. Its length is correct when it is easily found; the knee being in position, the tread should hang at about the boot heel.

> "With some riders, otherwise well-seated, the knees have a tendency to rise; with others whose thighs are well descended, the buttocks are disposed to leave the saddle. In the graceful seat *a la française,* the rider is on his buttocks and at the same time his thighs are well descended." (General L'Hotte)

In this seat at its perfection the legs are near the horse and vertical—neither to the front nor to the side nor to the rear. This position is the best; it is also the rarest and most criticized by those who can neither let their thighs down nor ride without stirrups. This position is an attribute of the privileged few to whom it gives security of seat, and control over the horse—he is so much better enclosed when the legs hang low—and, finally, it gives to them exactness in the use of their legs, due to the adherence which their verticality entails.

AIRS OF FANTASY

Rassembler
The base of the *haute école* is the *rassembler*. (See page 47.)

Piaffer
The *piaffer* is a rhythmic *rassembler*. To obtain it, halt the horse; demand the *rassembler*. Cadence is absolutely essential; it comes only when the horse is calm, and is a matter of slowing the time while elevating the forehand and hindquarters; this elevation is obtained by the application of the principle: hands without legs, legs without hands.

First, the hands demand lightness, then the legs alone act; hands receive the action produced by legs; legs immediately re-close. Let the horse work on his own as soon and as much as possible; encourage him to continue the cadence without rider's aids.

Generally the horse will throw his haunches to one side. James Fillis says he must be straightened by a sharp prod of the spur. Nothing is more contrary to good sense, especially with a nervous, high strung horse. This recommendation of a brutal prod of the spur abruptly changes the position of the out of line croup, but only for a moment; it does nothing towards remedying the cause which put it out of alignment. (I am always reverting to my hobby.) This brutal use of the spur is only violence, temper; it merely upsets the horse. Here, word for word, is General Faverot de Kerbrech's advice: "At the *piaffer*, if a horse traverses his croup [moves side to side, or to one side] he is resisting the hand. The traversed croup is the *effect*; resistance is the *cause*. The resistance must be destroyed by balancing the hand from right to left and from left to right—a sort of soft and regular vibration. This balancing of the hand is begun while the horse is at the *piaffer* and is continued as long as required—possibly for a long time—even if the horse backs a little; if he backs, diminish the hand effects. When lightness comes, backing ceases—the *piaffer* is correct."

Mabrouk at the *Piaffer*
Note particularly Captain Beudant's position: easy, graceful, secure; he is IN the saddle, not ON it.

If the horse is inclined to crow-hop (*saut de pie*[34]), repress him by half-halts. If a fore foot is planted in advance of the other, restrain the former by half-halts. If a hind foot is planted too far to the rear, it is brought under the mass by rider's leg on opposite side. Each horse requires different handling; tact is the horseman's guide.

PASSAGE

The natural *passage* is a slow trot characterized by lofty and dwelling action. The gait is natural with mules, asses, horses and some other animals. They take to it when feeling gay, when surprised, or when they strut and show off as a peacock.

The head is high—with mules and asses it is sometimes horizontal—the horse always carries it at the vertical, and

---

34 literally; jumps like a magpie.—*Editor's note.*

Nethou II at the *Passage*, Captain Beudant up

passages very slowly when he wishes to look his best (approaching a mare, etc.).

    The forelegs lifted high, knees rounded, seem to dwell in the air; the hocks bend as though moved by springs; the feet rebound from the ground as rubber balls. This gait is so beautiful, so graceful, that many horsemen consider it, even when poorly done, the criterion of the equestrian art. A poorly executed *passage* is no criterion; there is a world of difference between it and the perfect article. Moreover, to teach a horse to passage after a fashion is infinitely easier than to exhibit him smoothly at the gallop, supple and obedient, especially in the change of leg at every stride.

    There are many ways of teaching a horse the *passage*, for he must be taught it, though he has known it from colthood. I have heard these many ways vaguely cited, but have seen no demonstrations. I have been told that the horse must be put at counterchanges of hand, brought closer and closer together until finally he takes on two tracks one step to the right and one to the left, supported by a diagonal biped when changing direction. I have tried this method but did not persist; the exercise is too difficult when less than three steps are taken to each side.

My method is to push with my legs at each stride of the walk or trot, my hands remaining fixed. I do not know whether or not this method is generally used, but I do know that since adopting it I have always succeeded.

My first *passage* was on my mare La Gaieté, at Lunéville, with the 11th Cuirassiers. I do not know how I got it; I only know that I was groping about in the dark, and that such success as I had came purely by chance until I had the good fortune to study the method of General Faverot de Kerbrech.

In 1911, in the outdoor school of the 1st Chasseurs d'Afrique at Blida, I put a chestnut thoroughbred at the *passage* in less than one turn of the track. He was as heavy as a cart horse, and his terrifically rough gallop showed his utter lack of suppleness. Both his owner and I were stupefied. The horse was working magnificently; I waved my hand, and my friend, the owner who was on foot, tossed a stone at me, exclaiming, *"Mon Dieu,* he is going to make him do the Spanish trot!" However, not until at Rabat, while trying to get Captain Garineau's pure bred Arab, Laerte, to passage, did I sense the proper play of the aids to make the horse understand. Horsemen should bear in mind Newton's experience with the apple. Obscure incidents scarcely noticeable, if reasoned out, may bring undreamed of results.

Baucher and Comte d'Aure, who mastered the greatest equestrian difficulties, could doubtless have had their horses at the *passage* as quickly as they wished had not tradition, holding the *passage* to be the result of long and learned preparation, prohibited them from even dreaming of such procedure.

As a matter of fact, a *passage* is more readily taught an untrained horse than is a correct canter-depart. Of course, I do not refer to the perfect *passage*. General L'Hotte, speaking of the pure bred Arab, Neron, trained by Comte d'Aure, said:

> "He passaged, but not brilliantly; it lacked the distinctive, perfect regularity; moreover, this artificial gait was

beyond Comte d'Aure's practical realm—even beyond the principles which he professed."

Later Comte d'Aure trained and rode horses in the *haute école* in brilliant fashion.

It is fortunate that Baucher never thought of putting his horses to the *passage* immediately. Had he, he would have prescribed methods within the reach of all of us, and that would have been unfortunate. On the contrary, he was concerned only with horsemen who knew the charms of *lightness.*

Here is General Faverot de Kerbrech's description of the *passage:*

> "When the horse does the *piaffer* in place correctly, with cadence and suspension, he is asked for the *piaffer* while advancing; this is the *passage.*
>
> In the artificial *passage,* the horse advances very slowly, only about two or three inches at a step. To be regular, the *passage* must be very smooth and soft; its action is well rounded; the legs fold gracefully and in cadence. Its smooth, soft and rounded action is due to the concentration of forces, and to the *rassembler.* The *passage* is not a difficult gait for the rider to sit; it is not rough, and has nothing in common with the jerky, hard, disagreeable and uncomfortable trot which is sometimes called by the same name."

General L'Hotte says:

> "At its perfection, the rider may go by insensible gradations from the *passage* in place, the *piaffer,* to the most extended and energetic *passage,* and then return smoothly to the *piaffer;* running the entire ascending and descending scale without any brusque or abrupt changes in the horse's action. This exquisite perfection is attained only when the muscles are constantly active and supple. When the *passage* is carried to its greatest extension, the muscles while stretching remain pliant and supple: when shortened until it subsides into the *piaffer,* the hocks engaging under the

mass, still maintain their energetic play; the knees, though flexing roundly, are raised with a forward action as if the horse wished to gain ground to the front."

The *passage* is first obtained by pushing the horse to the front while he is at the *piaffer*. After he has learned the *passage* in this way, he is made to take it from the walk as follows: have him light; lower the hands; close the legs and receive the resulting impulsion on the hands.

By degrees he is induced to passage without aid of reins or spurs—as he does at liberty. (See impulsion, page 26) The artificial *passage* requires more tact and delicacy on the rider's part than does the natural *passage*. The artificial *passage* is not fatiguing to the rider; it may be executed without the use of the aids. On the contrary, the natural *passage* is uncomfortable and fatiguing to the rider, but when well-ridden it supples the horse; he becomes light; reactions become milder and smoother; the horse voluntarily slows the gait until it approaches and may even merge into the artificial *passage* described by General Faverot de Kerbrech. I believe the horses of the "Cadre Noir"[35] are generally trained in this way.

Horses entrusted to me for training, I teach the natural *passage*. With my own horses I take a much longer time. I first teach them the *piaffer,* whence comes all of the *haute école*.

The natural *passage* is far from the artificial *passage*. In the latter, all the horse's powers are submissive to and at the call of the rider. An expert rider can put an untrained horse to the natural *passage* almost immediately. In fact, we frequently hear the expression, "He is going to escape into the *passage*"—meaning that the horse, to defeat the rider, is adopting the natural *passage* as a defense. This gait is often very brilliant but is of no great use in training.

---

35   The celebrated corps of riding instructors at the French Cavalry School at Saumur, so called because of the black uniform.—*Translator's note.*

Captain Beudant Giving Mimoun a Lesson at the Extended Trot-Action!

The artificial *passage,* emanating from the *piaffer,* requires a much longer time to teach. At first, it, is usually less brilliant than the natural gait, but being the result of the absence of all resistance, the horse gives himself completely to the rider. He is light in mouth and haunches, perfectly balanced, his muscles relaxed; he is ready and aquiver to move in any direction at the slightest indication of the aids.

Exquisite at its perfection, the artificial *passage* expresses the talent of the trainer or rider.

The man who vaingloriously produces a *passage* in which the horse's hindquarters, under the shriveling effect of rider's legs, are painfully dragged along is unworthy of the name of horseman.

The really trained horse does the *piaffer* and the *passage* without rein-aids or leg-aids; his neck is high, head vertical, mouth light; all muscles relaxed, knees and hocks flexing in perfect cadence; he never advances except at the almost imperceptible indications of his rider.

Robersart II at Trot-to-Rear. A slight inclination of the rider's body to the front assists the horse in backing; his loins are relieved of part of the rider's weight.

THE TROT-TO-THE-REAR

Is backing while at the *piaffer*. A diagonal biped, having been in support for a moment, is carried a few inches to the rear of the other.

Hands act very lightly; heels or spurs give enough action to flex the hocks energetically. The horse's hind legs appear to begin the movement, not to be dragged along under the crushing weight of the mass.

The trot-to-rear may also be executed with longer strides, but is then less graceful, and more tiring to the horse.

THE *PASSAGE* ON TWO TRACKS

A difficult and very delicate maneuver. The horse is practiced in it by the means explained for work on the haunches.

Before undertaking the *passage* on two tracks, the horse should he thoroughly confirmed in two track work at the walk and trot. We should frequently revert to this basic work to prevent the horse from forming the habit of going into a *passage* when two-track work at the trot is demanded.

TheSpanish Trot, Captain Beudant on Mabrouk

EXTENSION OF THE FORELEGS

Place the horse with a wall or other obstacle on his right; the trainer standing on horse's left, slightly in advance of the shoulder obtains lightness by use of one of the left reins; while the horse is light, his left forearm is gently tapped with the whip at intervals of about one second. When the horse raises his left foreleg, stop, pet and reward him with rest. Similarly, the horse is induced to raise his right fore. The action of the rein must continue throughout the lesson to keep the horse light.

When the horse will raise his legs through the effect of the rein only (without use of whip), the trainer mounts. The horse, being at the halt and light, is made to raise a leg, the right for example, as follows: After a slight tension on the right rein in the direction of the left haunch, immediately close both legs; *when their pressure starts forward movement,* the hand opposes it by the same rein effect. This rein effect surcharges the left shoulder and frees the right. The willingness of the horse to raise and extend his right fore is in direct proportion to his obedience to the right rein. At the beginning the trainer may have to revert to the whip to make the horse understand. The least obedience must be rewarded. By requiring a little more and more each day, a full extension for as long a period as desired will result. The great difficulty is in obtaining a horizontal extension. I have trained two thoroughbreds and a French *demi-sang* [half-blood]. All three extended their legs horizontally. On the contrary, with Barbs I have obtained only one horizontal extension at the halt—with Robersart II.

THE SPANISH WALK

When the horse will extend each foreleg at the halt, begin to teach him the Spanish walk.

This air is simple enough to teach, but care and precaution are required to see that, the horse does not adopt the defense of raising and stiffening his back and pulling the extended foreleg toward him. The horse has difficulty at first in managing his hind legs which are alternately loaded when the forelegs are extended.

When a foreleg is well extended, the rider should close his legs and push the horse to the front. One step, reward; having obtained a step with the right fore extended, get one with the left; again reward, and so on. Little by little, the horse learns the Spanish walk, learns to maintain his lightness while performing at ever decreasing rein indications. The rein effects are exerted from below upward and from side to side.

The trainer, raising a hand slightly with each lift of a foreleg, accentuates that leg's extension by means of a half-halt. The rider will be well aware of a proper extension. He will have the sensation of a snap, as if the horse's knee were straightened by the release of a strong spring.

THE SPANISH TROT

When a horse has mastered the Spanish walk; when he is light and easy in that air, he is taught the Spanish trot. The horse being at the Spanish walk, and light, push him with the heels; at the same time move the hands from side to side to aid him in raising and extending his forelegs.

As the beats of the Spanish walk are brought closer and closer together, the speed is more and more increased.

Finally and imperceptibly, the beats are synchronized diagonally. The Spanish trot is born.

Notwithstanding the assertion of James Fillis, all horses are not easily trained to the Spanish trot. I have great difficulty in teaching it. The characteristic lifting of the hindquarters must he obtained by surprising the horse just at the right moment by a simultaneous application of the spurs.

When the Spanish trot is well executed, the horse is much let down; the cadence is very slow; the forelegs are thrown or SHOT forward, and very high. The Spanish trot develops the play of the shoulders, shoulder mobility, as no other exercise can.

THE EXTENDED TROT

The extended trot is characterized by the horizontal forward extension of the forelegs. It is best taught by going from the Spanish walk to the Spanish trot, and then stretching the latter until it becomes a frank, even fast trot: the forelegs are thrown horizontally to the front but not so high as in the Spanish trot.

The extended trot is a most brilliant gait. It is solicited by supports of the hands alternating with pushes of the legs.

Robersart II at Extended Trot. An exquisite picture showing the gait, and the seat *a la francaise* in all their classic beauty.

Robersart II at Canter-to-the-Rear

Canter [Gallop]-to-the-Rear

This is not a graceful movement. To obtain it, begin by habituating the horse to *rassembler* readily, to squeeze himself together *(pelotonner)*[36] while cadencing in place (from *piaffer)*; then put him at a slow canter which is slowed more and more, the horse on his own; finally, the horse is galloping in place but very vibrantly; he is bouncing like a ball, cadencing his action of his own accord.

While the forehand is in the air, the rider just HINTS at a backward step of no more than an inch or two.

The rider's legs are used very little and in this manner: after a few backward steps, obtained by the hands, then light taps with the calves to maintain the rise-and-fall of the canter. It takes a long time for a horse to learn the canter-to-the-rear; his strides are always extremely short. When a horse canters in place, well-cadenced, vibrantly, and with scarcely any rein effects, the canter-to-the-rear is easily obtained, but this preparatory canter-in-place requires much time and practice.

The canter-in-place is obtained by slowing the canter little by little. First, the hands act with extreme delicacy;

---

36 [Literally, wind up into a ball. *Editor's note*]

Canter on three legs. Captain Beudant on Mabrouk.
The canter on three legs, like the canter-to-the-rear, serves no useful purpose. The great masters of the past, to show their control and finesse, taught it to their horses; the moderns continue the custom.

when the canter is very slow, hands cease action; the role of the legs is mainly to insure vibrancy. The rider must be very calm; must often stop and reestablish balance.

Canter [Gallop] on Three Legs

This movement is very tiring to the horse, and like the canter-to-the-rear, is more of a *tour de force* than a gait. The canter on three legs is obtained as follows: put the horse at a very slow canter; halt and immediately make him raise the foreleg upon which he was leading; start again at the canter; halt, and again make him raise the same foreleg and depart at the canter while keeping the raised leg in the air.[37] The difficulty is in keeping the horse calm.

In all these extravagant and fantastic airs, trot- and gallop-to-rear, canter on three legs, etc., a great deal of impulsion is required; they also exact more complete obedience

---

37   Of course there *are* many halts and raisings of the foreleg before an attempt is made to depart on three legs. The interval between the raising of the leg and the depart is gradually shortened.—*Translator's note.*

Mabrouk: Looking his best, and proud of it.

of a horseman consists in having the horse assume attitudes and airs that he would adopt spontaneously if at liberty; then in seeming to efface himself—him the master. The horse, imagining himself free, warms to the imperceptible contact of the aids, and the ardor he displays, unconscious of a guiding hand, gives to his movements all their splendor.

The *éclat* [brilliance] which is so important in the *haute école* comes from the forehand. Consequently, the forehand must be trained to have the most elegant carriage possible. Nothing is so graceful as the swan neck, and the horse instinctively assumes it when he wishes to look his best. Impulsion and the position of the head come from the *petites attaques* and from the extreme *ramener*.

FINESSE OF THE HANDS. THE EXTREME *RAMENER*

The extreme *ramener* is first obtained by means of the snaffle reins as follows: cross them in the left hand, the little finger on the outside; place the right hand on the right rein; the left hand now closes forcefully, feeling the horse's mouth but not pulling. When lightness is manifest, the left hand follows the lowering movement of the nose until the horse's chin almost touches his breast. If the head, instead of ceding, tries to go to the front, the hand opposes it by contracting with great force, but never pulling on the reins. All this while legs have been closing, and finally the spurs come into play; they are held to the horse's sides until the jaw completely relaxes. When this relaxation occurs, the hand distinctly feels the complete vanishing of all resistance; the tongue plays with the bits, making them jump about and against the molars. If the horse is in a single snaffle, the characteristic sound of champing the bit is heard.

To confirm the horse, do all the school work at the extreme *ramener*—at walk, trot, and canter. Much backing at the walk, and then at the other gaits. Require the *piaffer* at the extreme *ramener;* quiet legs; use the spur if the horse does not obey the legs.

THE TRUE POSITION OF THE *HAUTE ÉCOLE*

The elevation of the neck combined with the extreme *ramener* gives and fixes the true position, which thereafter is never lost, even in the most difficult movements. The horse carries his tail high; his action is lofty and cadenced; his appearance has all possible brilliance.

RESULTS OF TRAINING

The *Haute École*

The annals of the *haute école* mention particularly:
Le Bonite, a horse trained by de Pluvinel and on which Louis XIII took his first lessons.

Le Florido, presented to Louis XIV by the King of Spain. Upon Le Florido, Cazeaux de Nestier, *écuyer ordinaire* of the royal stables, was represented as a model of equestrian position.

L'Andalou, with which d'Auvergne attained, at the natural gaits, a brilliancy then unknown.

Dentiste and Léos, the two favorite horses of Viscomte d'Absac, who, at eighty-three, rode them upon the eve of his death in 1827.

Effendi and Arc-en-ciel, belonging to Major Rousselet.

Norma, Laurent Franconi's horse.

Le Cerf, Le Sano, Maitre-de-danse, Marcellus, Endymion, Chasseur, Angevin, all belonging to Comte d'Aure. These horses and his exploitation of Tigris, Eylau and other thoroughbred stallions from the *haras* at Le Pin made him famous.

Kléber, Turban, Bloc, Picarde, Schandor, Stades, Partisan, Capitaine, Neptune, Buridan, Gericault and all the other horses ridden in public by the great Baucher.

Sabine, Laruns, Zégris, Sicambre, Glorieux, Domfront and Insensé, all belonging to General L'Hotte.

Germinal and Makir, James Fillis'.

Marseilles II, Iran, Menthol, Mademoiselle-d'Étiolles, trained in the *haute école* by Captain de Saint-Phalle.

And how many other horses have been and are being trained daily, and trained to perfection, by civilian and military horsemen!

I have never forgotten Le Paon belonging to Captain Benjamin, who was killed on his handsome and well-trained mare Loyauté; or the horses of General Faverot de Kerbrech when he commanded this regiment: Jambe-d'Argent, Bouton-d'Or and that terrible fool, Conspirateur, which, after being trained by the Colonel, was brilliantly ridden at Paris by Lieutenant de Corberon.

Equestrian art does not specialize in the *haute école*—far from it. True talent consists especially in training irascible and difficult subjects and making them agreeable for every day riding. Success in such work is the reason that the "gods," the *"écuyers"* of the *"cadre noir,"* are so admired.

> "Upon retiring to the reserves, General L'Hotte took Glorieux, Domfront and Insensé with him. He rode them daily in his small school in rear of his house. Often times he invited friends and officers of the garrison to see his horses work. These invitations were much sought after. Horsemen from Paris, Saumur, even from foreign lands, made pilgrimages to Lunéville to see the brilliant old master at work with his horses. They had that perfect lightness which was ever his goal. Even the most attentive spectator could not see a single movement of the aids.
> "In accordance with the General's expressed wish, his three horses were killed after his death. No one could ride them, and they were spared dreary old age. They are buried behind the cemetery wall at Lunéville near him who loved them." (*Un Officier de Cavalerie*, Appendix, last pages.)

The skeleton of Zégris is preserved at Saint-Cyr; that of Sicambre, at Saumur.

The fate of my unfortunate horses has not been so happy. They were much talked of in Morocco, but in Morocco there is not a great deal of knowledge about horses and riding. The opinions and compliments of the many "demi-connoisseurs" cannot be trusted. In fact, their compliments often fall obliquely, and even were they just, in welcoming them, one might run the risk of working to receive compliments. The only approbation a rider should covet is that of his horse. The horse is well aware of his rider's faults, and the latter can get a very true estimate of his own ability by the degree of obedience shown by his pupils, and his freedom from injuries.

Compliments have always embarrassed me because I do not know how to reply. When I rode, I did not want to be turned from what I was ever seeking—my horse's approval, his good humor and consequently his obedience.

The history of my horses describes very simply the application of the principles that have guided me. Their history is merely a collection of notes that I wrote, with no idea of publishing them, to M. Monod about the horses he had seen me work.

M. Monod knew me for years in Algeria, in Morocco, and in the Gharb. Later, when I commanded the remount district and the *haras* at Mazagan, I had the advantage of his opinion and advice on all that pertained to horses—breeding, raising, etc. I can never express the gratitude I owe this chief, so friendly, so learned, so wise. To him I owe, particularly, my horse, Mimoun, which taught me so much. Without the chief's encouragement I should have abandoned Mimoun instead of persisting and finally training him.

In detailing the circumstances of training, I am forced to introduce some rather flattering appreciations, but these are only evidences of the execution of the movements described. All the praise belongs to the precepts which have guided and directed my perseverance, and to my good horses, of which I speak feelingly now that I am physically unable to ride them.

ROBERSART II: The best, known of my horses in Morocco; a bay gelding, about 16 hands, foaled at Bourkika (department of Algiers), April 5, 1905, by the thoroughbred Robersart, out of the untraced Barb, Baronne.

His lightness almost readied that dreamed-of perfection described by General L'Hotte as contingent upon "the use a horse makes of those forces, and no other, required by the instant maneuver."

A spectator could call for any movement or combination of movements; Robersart II would solve the problem.

I do not believe that any other horse has ever done such sumptuous and difficult work in the *haute école*. The most extraordinary part of his exhibitions was the ease with which he passed at the call of his rider, and without time of transition, from one gait or air to another. He executed perfectly, always straight, successive counterchanges of hand on two tracks at the trot and gallop-to-rear.

Buckaroo Winning the *Barrienen Springen* Class at Köln, Germany, 1929
This jump is 6' 2". Captain Bradford, U. S. A., up.

Among some of his more difficult feats may be mentioned: changes of lead in gallop-to-rear; rocking his haunches[38] in the *piaffer* and in the trot-to-rear; passing, always without time of transition, and without apparent effect of the aids, from the change of leg at each stride to the *passage*, and inversely; from the *passage* to the Spanish trot, and inversely; from the *passage* to the extended trot, and inversely; from the gallop-to-rear or trot-to-rear to the *passage*, the Spanish trot, or the extended trot, and inversely.

When, just before parting with him, I rode him in the presence of a group of officers, he closed the *séance* [assembly] with the following exercises:

---

38   The horse raises his right hind, for example, as if to side-step to the left; when the right hind has been carried far to the left the rider brings it back by pressure of his left leg, which, at the same time, causes the left hind to be raised and carried to the right.- *Translator's note.*

At the gallop, on each leg, always maintaining the diagonal direction, he made:
1. A complete circle on the outside lead, with haunches to the inside.
2. A complete circle on inside lead, with haunches to outside.
3. Same work, changing leads at each stride (I believe it impossible to execute a more difficult movement).
4. Complete pirouette[39] on outside lead, head to inside.
5. Complete pirouette reversed[40], on outside lead, haunches to inside.
6. Many changes of leg in the gallop in the gallop-to rear, followed immediately by the trot-to-rear while rocking haunches, terminating with the Spanish trot.

After this exhibition, the Director of Remounts and Moroccan *haras,* whom no one can accuse of misstatements in order to be agreeable to me, wrote me from Rabat:

> "I am happy to tell you what pleasure it was to see Robersart work. His suppleness, his calm, his brilliancy were greatly admired by all who were so fortunate as to see the exhibition. I will testify that at Mazagan, on the 10th or 11th instant, I saw you put Robersart II through the following movements....."[41]

Robosart II's principal performances were:
At Kenitra, 9 November, 1913: having given a remarkable performance over the jumps in the show ring, he was ridden all day by me while organizing a native horse show. That evening, before General Lyautey, Comte Saint-Aulaire,

---

39   A turn in place, on the forehand; here it is done at the counter-canter!—*Translator's note.*

40   A turn in place, on the haunches; here it is done at the canter with counter-canter! —*Translator's note.*

41   Here are detailed the movements described above.-*Translator's note.*

Interallied Horse Show, Coblenz, 1920, Major Doak, U. S. A., and Colonel Melville, British Army.

the French minister, and other notables from Government House, I rode him in an exhibition of the *haute êcole*. He was then ridden seventy-five kilometers, and the next afternoon ran in a point-to-point race of 4,500 meters [2.8 miles], over country dotted with sand dunes. In spite of time lost by getting off the course—he was the only horse that did—he won by 172 meters, beating eleven horses of his own breeding (Algerian half-bred), nearly all of them ridden by officers who were good point-to-point riders.

> 1914—"Presented to His Majesty of the Riffian Empire, he gave an exhibition without equal. Not losing lightness for an instant, Robersart II, seeming to work at complete liberty, alternated without halts or intermediate gaits: the *piaffer*, the *passage*, the *passage* on two tracks half-turns (on forehands and haunches) at the *passage* trot-to-rear and gallop-to-rear, changes of

lead at each stride at the gallop, the Spanish walk, the Spanish trot, and the extended trot. Changes of gaits and airs were made without the slightest perceptible movement of rider's body, hands, or legs—without even a facial contraction to indicate effort." (Captain Dutertre, France Hippique, May, 1914)

At about that time General Piquemal, then colonel, saw the horse work on the *Aguedal* at Rabat. He immediately sent me the following letter signed by himself and six officers of cavalry, among them the Director of Remounts and Moroccan *haras* attesting:

"Robersart II's lightness, precision, accuracy and good humor in his remarkable exhibition of the *haute école;* particularly in the demi-pirouettes with alternate and rapid extension of each foreleg; in his work at the *passage,* Spanish trot, and extended trot. A horse of extraordinary suppleness, of a vibrant but perfect calm. In the airs derived from the *piaffer,* his hindquarters, very much engaged, showed a brilliancy comparing well with that of the forehand—proof of his perfect balance.
"As to Captain Beudant, who rode without stirrups throughout the exhibition, his position was admirable; well placed, well seated, hands low, legs falling naturally; not a movement, not even a gesture betrayed his will communicated to the horse by means imperceptible to spectators."

Some days later I received a letter from Captain Garineau, in which he said:

"I do not believe there ever has been another horse trained so nearly to perfection. Robersart II in his work seems to play completely free, and to pass from one gait or air to another at his own pleasure rather than at the dictate of his rider. How marvelous is his extended trot! At that gait he does not appear to touch the ground; a foreleg at its greatest possible extension seems continually in the air. To produce this extraordinary action, his thigh muscles contract to their limit and his hocks display astounding action.

"I have seen Robersart II give an exhibition of the *haute école* such as no other horse, at Saumur or anywhere else, ever equalled, *and then immediately jump, at an easy flowing gallop,* all the obstacles on the *Aguedal*—and there are some serious ones.

"I ardently hope to see him some day in Paris at the '*Etrier*,' or at Saumur at the cavalry school, to astonish our greatest masters."

Finally, Robersart II won this compliment from General Henrys. Captain Ciambelli, an officer of the General's staff, wrote:

"The General is pleased to say that never before in his career has he seen such mastery as yours. 'I have seen all the great masters of my day perform, among; them General L'Hotte,' he said to me, 'and not one of them left me with the impression of ideal perfection as did Beudant.'"

The day after a mobilization, made because of an expected outbreak of the Zemmours with Beni-Hassen, I rode Robersart II on a reconnaissance, the itinerary of which follows: up the left bank of the Fouarat, from its mouth to its source at Ras-el-Ain; thence around the forest opposite Monod, thence to Sidi-Yahia, crossing the Smento many times; at Lallo-Ito I stopped with the Caid Bouazza and returned via Camp Delmas, where I found a platoon of Spahis commanded by my kind and much lamented friend, the late Lieutenant Labitte. From Camp Delmas, via the railroad bridge over the Fouarat, guarded by a section of Zouaves, I returned to Kenitra.

Robersart II covered this enormous distance in the sand under a torrid sun between 5 A.M. and 1 P.M. He galloped most of the time.

A short while after leaving my hands my horses won renown in the races at Casablanca. Robersart II won, and Iris was third in a hurdle race. Whereupon Major Desfeux wrote me: "Your horses have been so perfectly trained that their new owner, who is far, very far from being a perfect horseman, with a little advice from me, put them through some airs of the *haute école.* They performed with such astonishing success that the owner was amazed.

> "In the hurdle race Robersart II won. The race was mainly between him and Velocity, and their duel was beautiful to see. At each obstacle Robersart's powerful jump gained him many lengths; then Velocity would catch him on the flat, and thus they fought throughout the race. Iris was third."

That same year Iris won five races in five starts on the flat, and was once second in a steeplechase. He continued to win for two years, in spite of the ever increasing weight he had to carry.

Robersart II's glorious victory at Casablanca was his swan song. He was too generous for the ignorant hands that tried to capitalize his noble qualities. Having been badly used for a long time, he was sold to the Nava circus for 7,000 francs.

Upon leaving the hospital at Casablanca in the Spring of 1920, I was questioned by his rider, a woman. She was disconsolate; the horse would not change at the gallop, or extend his forelegs in the Spanish walk, etc. She begged me to ride him for her. At first I refused on the plea that I was in civilian clothes, trousers, etc. Then, seeing my old horse saddled, I could resist no longer.

Poor Robersart II! He was pitiably lame and he bore on the bit—a thing he had never done with me Nevertheless, to the great joy of the woman, the grand old horse suppled up, and for the five minutes that I rode him he did repeated changes at the gallop and again showed the Spanish walk.

That was the last time I saw poor Robersart II!!

After misfortune forced me to part with them, Robersart II and Iris gave further proof of the soundness of the opinions of General Faverot de Kerbrech, that is to say of Baucher. The record of these horses establishes beyond doubt the fact that the work of the *haute école* takes nothing from a horse's speed and cross-country ability.

Iris, when I first got him, seemed utterly incapable of jumping, and no one at the Remount station dared try to make him jump. Yet, by riding him over varied obstacles —taking chances of getting some falls—and by training him in the *haute école*, I succeeded in making this small horse a good enough jumper to run in steeplechases.

My pleasure and joy over their victories have consoled me to some extent for the disappointment their owner caused by breaking his promise to give me "first call," if fate, becoming kinder, should have have permited me to buy them back.

Iris: A half-bred cherry bay gelding, 15 hands, foaled at Cardeilhac (Haute-Garonne) in 1910; by the Anglo-Arab, Loto, out of the half-bred Bécasse by Jarnac.

This horse is an example of the surprising changes which appropriate gymnastics make in conformation and gaits. His loins were very long and poorly attached; his hocks were way out behind him. When first brought to me, his croup was short and very light; he was shoulder-bound; his forearms had no reach; his gaits were short and broken, and he cut daisies in a terrible fashion. The veterinarian of the Remount committee who examined him described him thus: "Badly shaped, no weight carrier, better suited for harness, not suited for army service; commercial value 300 francs." An extremely nervous horse; he was used by a native in 1914 and 1915 to run match races at Arab fêtes. Upon leaving his hands, the horse had absolutely no describable gait. His two faults most difficult to correct were his four-beat canter and his continual head tossing.

I undertook his training as a two-fold experiment: first, to see if it were possible, in spite of his conformation, for him to be schooled passably well; second, I was especially anxious to find out if an animal with so little shoulder play and such weak loin muscles could be trained to execute those high school movements that require so much shoulder mobility and such great loin power.

As just stated, his loins were especially weak and he invariably galloped in four-beat time. Therefore, I taught him the gallop on three legs which demands great loin effort. I taught him the gallop-to-rear, which is said to require a very vibrant gallop; I taught him the Spanish trot, which necessitates great play of the shoulders that the forelegs may be extended and raised very high.

When I had finished, his work included the following movements:

First; Spanish walk—the ordinary Spanish walk, and one in which only one foreleg—either on demand—is raised and extended for any desired number of strides. Also, he would take any required number of strides at the Spanish walk with extension of one or both forelegs, alternated with the ordinary walk.

Second; *Piaffer*—slow, or rapid at will.

Third; *Passage*—varrying cadence and elevation at will; work on two tracks, including pirouettes and reversed-pirouettes; work on circle; repeated counterchanges of hand.

Fourth; Trot-to-rear.

Fifth; At, the gallop—complete pirouette; change of leg at will at each stride on a circle or straight line.

Sixth; Gallop-to-rear—either lead; on two tracks at gallop-to-rear on a circle or a straight-line.

Seventh; Gallop on three legs, either lead.

Iris, galloping on three legs, would pass from forward gallop to the gallop-to-rear, and inversely with full horizontal extension of a foreleg.

On September 21, in the presence of Lieutenant Petit and the non-commissioned officers of the Remount Depot at Mazagan, I rode Iris under the following conditions: I had just been discharged for the third time from the hospital at Casablanca, where I had spent seven months, ninety-two days of which I had been immobilized in a plaster cast. I was suffering from being hoisted up on Robersart II, who was a full hand taller than Iris; unable to wear riding boots, I rode in sandals, without whip or spurs.

Of this exhibition, Lieutenant Petit wrote:

"During this *seance* of the *haute école, my* cavalryman's heart was filled with admiration for that master horseman, Captain Beudant.

Bank and Bar
An officer at the Cavalry School, Fort Riley

"Painfully mounting, once in the saddle he asked permission to make a few turns of the ring to loosen his stiff joints; then he assumed the position of a master, and had Iris go through all the work just enumerated. You may well believe that there was no circus-work—no routine. Iris did just what he was asked to do, when he was asked, and as he was asked—nothing else. I admired the suppleness, the lightness, the good humor with which the horse, unridden for months, obeyed his rider. Not the slightest movement, not a gesture of the Captain betraying a command, could be noticed. Hands and legs immobile, Captain Beudant aroused my admiration.

"As to Iris he was simply marvelous—lively, full of energy, yet perfectly calm.

"Captain Beudant will permit me, as a horseman, to express my warmest praise of himself and his perfectly trained, exquisitely finished horse."

This letter had a postscript signed by the non-commissioned officers:

> "We also had the pleasure of seeing Captain Beudant on horseback, and we are happy to sign our names after that of Lieutenant Petit.
> "We must add, however, that hereafter when Captain Beudant rides for us, we hope he will tell us what aids he uses in the various movements. The Captain must repeat these movements many times while showing us the use of the aids, or else we can never distinguish which aids he is using."

There is astonishment at seeing no movement of my hands or legs while I am working my horse. There is nothing surprising in that. I am neither suppler nor more of a magician than anyone else. My position in the saddle comes from my principles of training: the horse must he light to spurs as well as to hands; no displacement of the seat, as an aid; allow the horse to work on his own once position is given.

The principles of riding and driving are similar. The carriage horse, when he has impulsion and knows his rein, requires no perceptible action or movements of his driver's hand to maintain a correct position. He himself maintains the position. But the same driver perched on a cart would cut quite a different figure whipping a horse while restraining his advance.[42]

MABROUK: A Barb, gray mottled with roan, 15-1h.h. by Cheddi, a Barb, out of the Barb, Messaouda; foaled in 1907 at M. Bedouet's *Haras* de Saint Georges. (Constantine)

Impossible to ride in ranks, the 3d Spahis left the horse with Lieutenant Garinoau, who later brought him to Batna, but could not use him. At Batna he was known as a "fool"; was seldom ridden—and then only by the younger officers as a stunt.

---

42 The author is contrasting the difficulties of the rider and of the driver; the simile is intended to describe the tact and skill required for the *piaffer* or other movement in place.—*Translator's note.*

The horse was brought to my attention through M. Garineau's report on him to the colonel commanding the subdivision. At that time Mabrouk was very restless; he would not stand still; was in a run-down condition due to his nervousness and disordered gaits. When Lieutenant Garineau learned that I was riding Mabrouk in *haute école* he wrote me: "My old friend Mabrouk, hot tempered Mabrouk, become a horse of the *haute école,* I can't believe it! You are—" etc.

Major Charles-Roux who knew the horse, having tried him at Batna, could not believe his own eyes when I rode Mabrouk with him at Mazagan.

Mabrouk became a good outdoor horse and a strong jumper. Unfortunately his gallop though fast was poor. My greatest difficulty was to induce him to cross small ditches quietly. At Batna he had become obsessed with fear of a drain or ditch because a staff officer in trying to longe him over a ditch had injured one of his knees.

One day during the Remount colt show, Major Charles-Roux sent for me. Robersart II requiring no work that day, I had purposely ridden Mabrouk to the show, thinking that the Major, who knew how nervous the horse was, would not ask me to ride him in public. I was mistaken. I had to give an exhibition in front of the grand stand.

Although the commandant of the Arab militia had forbidden his men access to the track, I expected to see Mabrouk, in a single snaffle, lose his head and take me for a ride. To my great surprise, nothing of the sort happened. In spite of the order of the commandant, the militia, firing their rifles, charged mounted past me three times. Three times I was able to keep Mabrouk perfectly quiet, and after the smoke cleared away I gave a much applauded exhibition in the *haute école,* including the Spanish trot, gallop on three legs, etc. Only the doctors and a few others knew what torture I suffered during that exhibition.

I shall treasure always, as a precious possession, the letter of appreciation from Major Charles-Roux, incomparable leader with a brilliant future, who met a hero's death at Ferrières Wood, 25 October, 1918, while leading his regiment, the 11th Algerian Rifles, against the enemy. He is mourned by all—his soldiers, his officers, and his seniors.

Nethou II: Iron gray gelding, 15-3h.h., an Anglo-Arab, by Velasquez, out of Neyère.

A winner of 11,300 francs on the tracks of the Sud-Ouest, he had been bought for 16,000 francs at Toulouse, 29 October, 1918, and later rejected by the *Haras de France* as unfit for breeding purposes. In spite of this rejection, the Purchasing board at Merignac bought him for 3,000 francs for stud purposes in the Riff.

While examining a draft of thoroughbreds unloaded at Casablanca on 19 January, 1916, the Director of Remounts and Riffian *Haras* considered Nethou too long and too dissimilar in conformation to breed to native mares. His estimate was correct. An hour after the inspection of the stallions just unloaded, I met General Henrys, then C. in C., and he asked me to select a charger for him. I told him of the Director's remarks about Nethou II, and gave my estimate of the horse. A few hours later Nethou II was in the General's stables and his training had been intrusted to me.

At first Nethou was unbelievably awkward over varied ground. He was also stubborn and balky. He would whirl, head-to-tail, with the characteristic suddenness of that defense when the habit has been contracted on the race track.

Although he was in very poor condition after a six-week stay in the veterinary infirmary, he became a model charger within a few months, remarkably manageable with one hand at the fastest gaits; he jumped high and with a great spread over the jumps.

General Henrys returned to France and Nethou was turned over to Major Rastoin. I believe the horse later reverted to his stubborn ways.

Nethou was difficult to set in his high school work on account of his short neck and long loins. He carried all of his weight on his shoulders which were poorly muscled. The saddle continually slipped to the front. His weight had to be brought to the rear, his poll elevated, and his head brought to the vertical without lowering it, or shortening the neck. When finished, Nethou changed leads at every stride; his *passage* was brilliant; his *piaffer* absolutely in place, without hand-or leg-aids; his action was big and round. He earned well the name "Splendid Nethou" which General de La Garenne gave him.

In 1919 he was in the Remount at Boucheron; his classification as "unfit for breeding," if erroneous, was a great loss to Moroccan horses.

EMBAREK: He deserves little attention. A chestnut gelding, Moroccan, bought at Taza by a captain of the 127th Territorials. Embarek became the terror of the orderly who rode him. The horse was turned over to me 23 February, 1917. I was en route to Rabat, and on 3 March, led him to Casablanca. There the doctors decided to put me in a plaster cast, but before going to the hospital I rode Embarek in the presence of Captain de—. Then the captain mounted him, and at my direction put him to the *passage* and to the canter. The young officer was so pleased that he bought the horse and his outfit on the spot. The horse was afterwards sold to the Remount and became an officer's charger.

MIMOUN: Dark chestnut gelding, crooked list, one front and both hind fetlocks white, 15-3½h.h., foaled in 1915.

When I bought him in 1919 at Settat, his topline though long, was good enough; his chest was excellent; his neck very short, his hocks curby and gummy, hindquarters light, breeches narrow; in general, instead of being wedge-shaped from rear to front—the conformation admired so much by the English—his chest was very large and his barrel tailed off to knife-edge quarters.

I had him gelded because his neck threatened to become enormous; its crest was extraordinarily thick, a characteristic of Moroccan horses.

In all my twenty-eight years in Arab countries, I have never seen an animal so timid as Mimoun. When being delivered to me after purchase, his eyes had to be covered to get him across a small gully, and then he crossed only with much persuasion from a club. He was afraid of dwarf palm trees, of plants, even horses or mules he met during a ride. In a word, he was afraid of everything except camels.

I described him in a letter to M. Monod as follows:

"An extremely slack horse, scared by the least noise or at the sight of objects which other horses never notice.

"Any change of light, shadows, or the sudden appearance of the sun, a horse or an ass grazing far away absolutely terrifies him. I shall probably never succeed in making him bold.

"Hacking, he is very disagreeable, always jumping at a noise, or shying at some object. I have never ridden a horse so lacking in impulsion. When I dismount, his head drops to his knees, his eyes close, and it is almost impossible to make him budge—it would take a wagon whip. I have always trained my horses to move forward at the touch of the whip on the barrel. I have had to give up this practice with Mimoun—he is so insensitive.

"When not mounted, if the cut of the whip is hard enough he will kick or make a leap to the front; then stop flat-footed and sprawl again. His muscles have no elasticity; he seems even to resist his own inertia like a cart horse falling back into his breeching to hold the cart.

"Mounted, he reacts to the spurs in the same fashion; moving, all action dies when my legs cease driving. At first I attributed his heedlessness to weakness or sickness. I no longer do, but I am not less discouraged. I am particularly disheartened at my utter inability to make him trot, a gait he seems incapable of taking.

"I think the solution of the problem is to muscle and develop his croup without overworking his hocks; to teach him to trot; to elevate the poll and bring his head to the vertical without lowering his already too short neck. He is Nethou II minus that most important factor—Blood! Mimoun has no shoulder muscles; the saddle is always on his neck.

"I am much concerned about his weak hocks. The country around Settat is hard on horses' legs and joints. There are no level spots. The roads have no side paths for horses, and are literally covered with stones. But the worst

Captain Gerhardt, U. S. A. An excellent cross-country jumping seat. The rider is secure but easy. He is with the horse. The stirrup is short enough to allow the rider to get out of his saddle, but long enough to permit use of his legs in case of a peck, a stumble, or a possible refusal.

feature is the soil; when wet from rains or from the heavy dews, it balls in horses' feet, a condition extremely tiring and dangerous to a horse with bad hind fetlocks and weak hocks.

"My horses, Robersart II, Iris, and Mabrouk, were all naturally very nervous, yet their calm astonished all who saw them work. I made them calm by the *effet d'ensemble.*

"If by the *rassembler* and *petit attaques,* I succeed in giving Mimoun a little of the brilliancy and something of the stamp of my old horses, I shall have shown once more the excellence of General Faverot de Kerbrech's method. According to him, 'the *effet d'ensemble* calms, mollifies, rules; the *rassembler* awakes, animates, incites action, gives life and brilliancy.

"In any case I am discouraged, for the horses I like best are the nervous ones, particularly mares, for instance my excellent mares Kakta and Hamia, which you heard of in Algiers.

"It is on account of Mimoun that I am restrained from citing your appreciation of my other horses. Nothing pertaining to the hippic sciences is unknown to you, and horsemen are constantly bringing you their problems. I doubt, however, if any of those gentlemen, so full of theory, have ever given you a problem like Mimoun; viz., a very weak horse, ill-suited to saddle, that must be taught natural gaits which he has never possessed. Those gentlemen have not been able to show you high school work with a young horse, lacking in blood, and so unsound in hocks as seemingly to preclude even hacking. Surely such a problem may rightly be termed an *equestrian difficulty*."

Whatever he may have been, Mimoun is now, in 1922, a big horse, nearly 16 hands, with energetic action in his high school work. His conformation is entirely changed; his shoulder muscles are well developed and hold the saddle in place. There is no sign of a bursal enlargement on his hocks.

Prior to Mimon's exhibition in the *haute école* at a Remount colt show, I wrote Colonel Monod and asked for his opinion of the horse's work. Both letters are here reproduced.

"Settat, 6 May, 1920.
"A horse is like a violin; first it must be tuned; once tuned— then it must be accurately played." (Rousselet.)

"Dear Colonel:

"The honor you do me in coming to see Mimoun work gives me great joy. Your opinion, authoritative and sovereign on all matters pertaining to the horse, will appraise definitively—and I dare hope favorably—the ideas I have expressed upon the training of the riding horse in *haute école* or for outdoor riding.

"The question is very plain.

"It is generally held that success in the *haute école* requires a carefully selected horse; that the subject must approximate the ogival, long-line type, with knees and hocks rather high, a well-muscled top line, the loins well rounded and strong.[43]

"Others, on the contrary, want the prospective *haute école* horse high in front, made like a cock. All demand that their model have impulsion, springy gaits and good natural balance.

"I am not so particular. I do not believe that a horse of special conformation is required. On the contrary, I think the rider should be concerned mainly with himself. Let him strive earnestly to make himself understood, and with calm. Let him beware of asking a *fagged out horse for work of precision.* The horse must be fresh for a difficult lesson; he should take it as a game mixed with rest and reward.

"For the *haute école,* the thoroughbred is immensely superior to all other horses, and the best type is that of the powerful galloper—neck long, back and loins short, croup high, knees and hocks well let down. But in my opinion an animal deficient in the make-up of a great galloper can be made into a creditable high school horse. The work of the *haute école* gives to the natural gaits an elasticity, a freedom, an openness, all without inconvenience or fatigue, that no other method can approach.

"M. Eloi Josselme, whom I have just quoted, is quite right in saying, in *France Hippique,* 31 January, 1913: 'The work of the *haute école* does not spoil or injure a horse in any way, for any service. On the contrary, a horse capable of the greater tasks can certainly perform the lesser ones. The *haute école* balances and perfects him for all service; gives him carriage. The judicious gymnastics for his entire musculoskeletal system and the suppling of all parts of his body strengthen the horse, and consecutively, develop a surprising facility for ordinary riding.'

"Mimoun, a large, coarse, cold blood Moroccan, opposed inertia to every attempt to move him. He, therefore, is exactly opposite—in temperament, in energy, in power, in musculature—to the horses you have seen me ride. He anchors me still deeper in my conviction that all horses—

---

43   M. Eloi Josselme, *France Hippique,* 31 January, 1913.

except those ruined by man—may be made as supple and brilliant under saddle as at liberty.

"Robersart II had a fine neck and good withers, but his low croup did not belong to his forehand.

"Iris was higher behind than in front. His loins were long and poorly attached. His neck and shoulders were short, and he was heavy-headed.

"Mabrouk was well conformed. All three were very nervous.

"Mimoun's head is badly attached. His neck is short, his hocks poor. He lacks blood, nervous energy—all the general attributes of a good riding horse. Yet he has become a robust servitor. He is a good feeder. His feet and legs are sound. His temperament is kind.

"The training of each of these four horses was based on the same principle. I ask, my dear colonel, your sincere opinion upon the results of this training, and upon the method which obtained the results, a method that anyone can apply.

"Mimoun is now completely changed; his croup is much larger *(piaffer)*, his shoulders much freer (Spanish walk), his hocks have improved, and he now has an even, regular trot. Besides, I have taught him some movements whose execution must convince connoisseurs that in spite of his lack of blood and poor saddle conformation, he has acquired good gaits out of doors; that he gives his all to his rider to do with as he wishes. Mimoun, under the saddle, acts like a horse at liberty. At the ordinary gaits his neck is horizontal—a little higher at the trot and the gallop. 'On parade' his head and neck are lofty, his action high; he shows all possible brilliance. It seems as though his neck has been lengthened by the *rassembler.*

"*More particularly his work includes:*
1. Natural gaits and airs (*passage,* change of leg at the gallop).
2. Artificial airs (*piaffer,* Spanish walk with extension of forelegs, two tracks, reversed pirouettes, changes of leg at every stride, trot-to-rear).
3. Many exercises contrary to the laws of

International Horse Show at Nice
Captain Calvi (Italy) on Firman,
winning the *Prix du Comité des Fêtes et Sports*

mechanics (two track at counter gallop, reversed pirouettes at counter gallop, changes of lead while at the gallop on two tracks without changing direction, etc.).

"To go into greater detail:
1. Walk—At a cadenced walk, he slows it while lengthening the stride; he accelerates it while shortening the stride, and he will do either at the bidding of his rider. I have never heard of any one even dreaming of a horse doing this. I am inclined to believe that this 'march of fantasy,' in spite of its simplicity, is *the best proof of the rider's complete possession of the horse.*
2. *Piaffer*—Haunches to the right, then to the left, often repeated.
3. *Passage*—Pirouettes and pirouettes reversed.

Passage on two tracks, counterchanges of hand.
4. Trot-to-rear.
5. Spanish walk—Extension of one foreleg only, the right, for example; alternate extension of the forelegs; extension of the same foreleg for any number of required strides alternating with extension of the other for the same number of strides. These airs are interspersed at will by strides at the ordinary walk. The forelegs are shot to the front.
6. Work at the gallop:
A. Gallop on two tracks.
B. Circles, half circles and counter changes of hand on two tracks.
C. Same as B, at false gallop.
D. Counterchanges of hand on two tracks, changing leads in the air so that the horse is always at the false gallop.
E. Counterchanges of hands on two tracks without changing leads.
F. Same movements as in D and E but without gaining ground to the front, horse always parallel to original direction.
G. Being at gallop, Mimoun stops, pirouettes on either foreleg, the right for example, while holding the left [front leg] extended perfectly straight and horizontal; then, at the indication of the rider, he reverses his forelegs, pivoting on the left and extending the right; and finally, bringing the right to the ground, he immediately takes the gallop with the left lead. *This alternate support and extension of a foreleg indicates complete mastery of rider over horse.*
H. On a straight line he carries his haunches from one side to the other without changing leads.
I. Change of lead on two tracks without changing direction.
J. On a circle; with inside lead and with haunches to inside, he changes hands without changing leads and keeps the haunches to inside while galloping on outside

lead; inversely, he carries haunches to outside while on outside lead and keeps them there after changing hands.
K. Ordinary pirouettes.
L. Ordinary pirouettes at counter gallop.
M. Reversed pirouettes.
N. Reversed pirouettes at counter gallop.
O. Change, smooth and quiet from the *piaffer* to the most extended *passage,* then to trot-to-rear; return to *piaffer.*
P. Beginning of the Spanish trot.
Q. Trot regular, and extended. This is the gait I am happiest to have obtained because it is a natural gait, and one at which Mimoun was particularly inapt.

"These various exercises are executed in any desired order."

E. Beudant.

"My dear Beudant:

"My sincere opinion, first, on the results of Mimoun's training; second, on the method which produced them; here it is:

"From a slack, flabby horse, common, with short lines, poorly muscled, you have made and shown mounted a supple and brilliant horse, lightly responding to your demands, and demonstrating—notably in the foreleg extensions of the Spanish walk and in the *passage*—a surprising vigor and energy. All of his high school work—two tracks, pirouettes, changes of leg at each stride, work at the false gallop—was executed without apparent effort, and at the scarcely perceptible indication of the rider.

"The gymnastics of the work have considerably developed the muscles of his shoulders and thighs. The carriage of his head has vastly improved, and it now comes to the *ramener* as lightly and as easily as the finely attached head of a thoroughbred.

"His hocks, formerly rough and gummy, have cleaned up, and his hock action has improved. A method which produces such results; which improves the horse's conformation; which brings him to the end of training with legs cleaner than at the beginning; which leaves the impression that the horse works without effort, in freedom and lightness, is surely the method to follow—the only method.

"You know how to tune your violin, to play it true, even brilliantly. Only an artist, and with an instrument like Mimoun; only the virtuosos of equitation can pretend to a training so perfect."

Th. Monod,
Vetérinaire Principal, Director of Troop Veterinary Service, Chief of Breeding, French Remount Service in Morocco.

Suddenly I have had to abandon the two tracks, the *piaffer*, and high *passage*. Now I ride Mimoun on solitary quiet rides for health in pine woods, dreaming, sometimes with sadness, of hopes blasted and gone awry. Once I anticipated ending my days with the Cavalry among horsemen and beautiful horses.

To prove that something could be done, in spite of conformation, *in spite even of lack of blood*, I put this horse (Mimoun) to the gallop-to-rear; to the extended trot without first teaching him the Spanish trot—contrary to the generally adopted schedule for high school training.

I went contrary to custom in teaching Mimoun the gallop-to-rear. Baucher, the master of the art, said for this *tour de force* that the horse must gallop very, very slowly, on his own, and he added: "It is essential that the gallop be very vibrant." I have never demanded a vibrant gallop from Mimoun. He will gallop very slowly, but his gallop in place, and gallop-to-rear, like his regular gallop, are almost four beat gallops—the beats of his diagonal biped are not synchronized. Certainly no four beat gallop can be vibrant.

Mimoun does the extended trot with extraordinary brilliancy. Each hind foot is lifted hock-high, while its diagonal shoulder completely unfolds to thrust the forearm forward. Forthwith, it seems that a powerful spring released in his knee shoots his foot as straight and as far to the front as possible. This alone, this extended trot in rapid cadence, is enough to make my horse magnificent. Yet it will have no recompense other than my personal satisfaction; the brilliance of Mimoun will remain forever unknown to those who could appreciate it.

Purely as a fantasy, in addition to the unnatural way he slows and accelerates the walk, I have taught Mimoun to do two track work, pirouettes and pirouettes reversed at the Spanish walk. He passes from a Spanish walk in which each foreleg is shot energetically to the front, to a Spanish walk in which each foot is planted with all possible force. He will do either of these Spanish walks at a simple aid indication. I have taught him all of these airs by the sole use of hands and legs—without use of whip and with no work on foot. Moreover it is very simple and not at all difficult.

I am a little curious to see theorists explain mathematically just how I should have gone about it. I should like them to calculate to my satisfaction just what I did to obtain these results.

Many horses that I have ridden without training them at all—in the proper sense of that word—have demonstrated conclusively the uselessness of scientific theories in training a horse in the natural gaits, especially in the *passage,* which all horsemen consider the pinnacle of the education of a riding horse. I will mention some of these untrained horses:

KORAN II: The best of them is Koran II, owned when I rode him, by Captain Ciambelli, a staff officer of the C. in C. Captain Ciambelli wrote me:

> "My dear Captain Beudant,
> "Allow me to express my grateful admiration of the masterly lesson in advanced equitation which you were kind enough to give me.
> "In spite of your great reputation as a horseman, I must admit that I could never have believed you capable of putting my horse, Koran II, at the *passage* in one lesson. Yet you did it, and in front of my very eyes,—without any prior supplings, and after only a few minutes at the walk and trot: Marvellous!
> "Thank you again.
> "Sincerely yours, etc."

After Captain Ciambelli left for the Western front many

officers from the embassy and in the vicinity of Fez rode Koran II—among them Lieutenant P. L. If a single one of them, after applying the learned combinations ordinarily considered indispensable in teaching a horse the *passage,* had succeeded after several months of effort, he would have passed, at least in his own estimation, for a horseman of talent.

KENITRI: An atrocious little dog of which a friend had asked my opinion. I had him ridden by a non-commissioned officer from the Embassy, who as soon as he mounted exclaimed: "My God, Captain, this thing is a mule!" I then straddled him to go from Rabat to Salé (two and one-half miles); an hour later, upon my return, Kenitri, without a wet hair and with no sign of abuse, passaged regularly, and as well as his villainous conformation and lack of blood would permit. He was lame to boot.

HASSANI: The non-commissioned officer mentioned above wrote me with reference to Hassani:

> "I have many times ridden Hassani, the gray Algerian that Captain Beudant asked me to break. He was intolerable on account of his vicious head-throwing; besides, he was so weak that no effort whatever could be asked of him. Captain Beudant rode him in single snaffle from Temara to Rabat (seven and one-half miles). I was amazed when I saw the horse, absolutely green, without training of any kind, at the *passage.* During the ride the Captain on five or six different occasions put him to that gait without the horse showing the slightest ill humor."

VOLTIGUER: This horse, from the Riffian Guard, I put at the *passage* while awaiting his owner, my host, on the Aquedal at Rabat.

The old Baron de Vaux, not to be confounded with the author of *Écuyers et Écuyers* (1893), wrote me with reference to these horses:

> "As to Kenitri, Voltigeur and Hassani, I am glad to attest that you succeeded in obtaining from these three

horses the first time you rode them—and in a single snaffle—a *passage* which, while not lofty, was nevertheless characteristic and of perfect cadence.

"Never before in my long career have I seen a like result—a result all the more astonishing because attained with subjects whose conformation seemed to preclude all hope of success."

DRAGON (EX-UHLAN): A bay stallion from the Mazagan depot, 15-1h.h., five years old, by the Arab-Barb, Ibech.

Almost as insensitive to spurs as to legs; to the hands he opposed his stiff jaw, and in addition, the enormous weight of his head and fleshy neck. Like all other Remount stallions, he had had absolutely no training under the saddle.

Upon my arrival at the depot I wanted to show the Director of Remount Service that, contrary to his opinion, a stallion could passage without laming his hocks. I rode Dragon at the review held for the Director. A quarter of an hour later I showed him the horse at the *passage.* I put Dragon at it several times—sometimes from the walk, sometimes from the slow trot.

BAUDRES: I had ridden Dragon before showing him to the Director. I feared that someone might suspect that I had secretly trained the horse. Accordingly, I asked Corporal de Paix de Coeur, who was on duty, to have any horse whatsoever saddled, provided he was notorious for his lack of training. The corporal had Baudres saddled for me. Baudres was an immense four year old Barb stallion with a rubber neck that was weak and flabby beyond imagination. I mounted him at just 4 o'clock p.m. and when I returned at 4:20 p.m. he passaged regularly, even brilliantly five or six different times. The horse did not have a wet hair, not a welt, not a trace of punishment.

MAZAGAN: I am boasting neither of equestrian talent nor of horse knowledge; I am simply expressing some ideas which are my own and which I have not the least thought of imposing on others. Yet I cannot refrain from condemning the pretensions of those who profess to believe that they can manage and care for a horse as a mechanic guides and repairs a motor car. Here are some facts to consider. When I took command of the 3d Remount district, I found at the Mazagan depot six stallions which were extremely difficult, even dangerous, to handle. Three of them, Mazagan, Malek, and Ali-Baba, each required two strong men to lead him. A man would get on each side of the horse and at some distance from him; a snaffle rein, passed through its opposite ring, prevented the horse from jumping on either man.

If I am hostile to complicated, abstruse, arid theories, I have nothing but respect for certain principles, the first being: "The horse must obey his rider as the dutiful son obeys his father." To obtain this obedience it is necessary to show a resolute authority, especially with animals become ill-natured and vicious. True authority is calm force, judiciously employed without injuring, without paining the horse. This calm force succeeds in conquering his morale; blows merely exasperate and madden him.

The best way to conquer an unruly horse is first to discipline him on the Charvet[44] longe, and then, mounted, to apply the *effet d'ensemble* on the spur. (see EFFET D'ENSEMBLE ON THE SPUR)

Ali-Baba was the most to be feared, because he would jump upon a man; he was difficult and dangerous to ride. If he succeeded in throwing his rider, he would jump on him and viciously bite him. I alone, without an assistant, took the horse, and he made not a shadow of resistance. At the succeeding weekly veterinary review all six of these horses were shown in hand, standing and moving, with no more concern than were the other stallions at the depot.

The most interesting of these horses was Mazagan, a dark dappled gray, by the pure Arabian, Bul-Bul. Mazagan

---

44   The Charvet longe is a method no longer in use. It involves using a version of a Colbert rein while lunging. The cord is passed from the inside bridoon, up over the back of middle of the neck (from inside to outside) then through the two rings of the curb bit, then through the throatlatch, and to the hand of the handler. [not recommended for many reasons the least of which is the cord does not easily release due to multiple points of friction thus being dangerous in unskilled hands.] Described here for historical interest, not as a training recommendation.—*Editor's note.*

was the most elegant of all the depot stallions. When shown in hand he would twist in all directions, trying to strike or bite his handlers. He would not walk—was always galloping, or rather bounding, kicking at each bound. When, on rare occasions, he did trot, he limped so badly that he was at once returned to the stables.

Several times I had expressed my admiration for Mazagan to M. F.— the veterinarian, on his Thursday visits of inspection. "Out of curiosity, why not ride him?" he said to me. I had been much concerned over the horse's lameness; he was in a pitiable condition. The cause of his inability to trot was apparently in his lumbar region which seemed to hurt him whenever he tried to trot.

"It could not be said," M. F.— continued, "that you made him lame, for we have been treating him for lameness ever since he arrived at this depot." M. D.—, M. F.'s successor, insisted, almost demanded in the interest of science, that I send the horse to his hospital for observation. He thought the pain in the horse's loins was probably due to a trypanosoma. I am glad I did not follow his advice. I rode Mazagan. He limped; but by supporting with the reins the shoulder on which he nodded; by closing my legs, which he obeyed, thanks to some lessons with the spur, I succeeded in preventing the limp at the walk and trot. At the gallop it was more difficult; his gallop was very broken, and I did not attempt that gait for some time. Finally, when I did try to gallop him I had to stop; he seemed about to fall on his nose at each stride. He would not take the right lead, and kicked madly at any attempt to force him.

However, in about one month I was able to write to my friend, M. D.— "Now Mazagan never thinks of limping; his walk is unusually bold and rapid; he trots well and is light and agreeable to ride. Only his gallop remains defective, but it is improving each day. What is most astonishing about the horse is his quiet, sweet temper. I ride him through all the narrow streets of the town, through crowds of native children, who, accustomed as they are to Moroccan horses, are always under his feet or swinging to his tail. Like an old timer, he is indifferent to all shocks. Soldiers at the depot, who dared not even hold him for me some days ago, now laugh at their former fear. The first time I rode him in the rain, when put to the gallop, he kicked at my rain cape; two attacks with the spurs effected a complete cure. Now he pays no attention to the cape, regardless of how it flops around in the wind. My greatest difficulty has been to prevent him travelling sideways—carrying his haunches to the right—especially at the *piaffer.* Perhaps he has some defect in conformation which causes this carriage. Nevertheless this recently sick, afflicted, chronically lame animal, unfit for all service, is now a handsome saddle horse. In his work he evinces no pain; he limps no more over rocky going than in sand—he does not limp at all."

I have exaggerated nothing. For a long time I have had my opinion about horses said to be lame in the lumbar region. Grillade, my first charger, the veterinarians said, was suffering from lumbar pain. No one but me could ride her; she never kicked with me, novice that I was. Maybe it was because of my ignorance. When I left some months later she had been ridden by every man in ranks—and without kicking, in spite of the crupper and other paraphernalia of those days, which she would never bear until I took her.

WIMBLEDON : I could cite many such cases, but let this one suffice. Early in 1914, M. Durand de Villers had bought from M. Delapalme a handsome thoroughbred by Launay. The horse was an inveterate kicker and was sold because of this trait.

M. Durand de Villers having asked me to discipline and correct the horse, I rode him for the first time on the Rabat road, in company with the Director of *haras.* Wimbledon went remarkably well at all gaits, including the extended gallop. On my return to Kenitra, I rode him at walk, trot and gallop past his stable, and he made no effort to kick.

Captain P—, who was about thirty pounds lighter than I, and a very good rider, often rode Wimbledon, and the horse never ceased kicking, although he kicked less viciously when returning to stables than when going out. Under the circumstances, it was concluded that Wimbledon did not kick with me because I used a deerskin numnah [saddlepad]. I then, for more than a month, rode him with an English saddle over a leather numnah, and finally with an ordnance saddle. He made no attempt whatever to kick.

After passing into other hands, Wimbledon reverted to his villainous habit of kicking, which the veterinarian said was due to a spavin.

A farmer in the Gharb kept this poor beast in a stable for four days without water or feed—not even a wisp of straw. On the fifth day he rode him with a bull-whip, galloping and beating him unmercifully. I do not know whether he broke the horse or not. I do know that he arrived at the Embassy stables looking like a skeleton and with a coat like a goat's.

Lieutenant G—, who bought him, had the lame hock fired, but once over the firing, the handsome chestnut reverted to his former state. He was tried in harness, and when I last saw him had broken up many buggies. In 1921 I learned that he had entered the army. The Remount Service refused to assign him to Lieutenant Hugo, commanding the Riffian Squadron, and finally sent him to the Moroccan Spahis at Salonika, where he was used by Major Holtz.

These horses always kicked w i t h other riders; they did not kick with me. Could their kicking have been due to spavin, or kidney trouble? I am no cure for those ailments. I am, or at least I was, as other humans—neither more nor less of a devil. The horses did not kick with me because I made no mathematical calculations and was not imbued with my science. I simply avoided fatiguing and annoying them by useless and futile "effects."

FABRICIUS: The handsomest horse ever in Morocco, a dappled gray stallion, five years old, 16 hands; by the Anglo-Arab Cadi, out of the Anglo-Arab Fleur-de-Lys.

Fabricius was imported from the Midi 19 January, 1916, and sent to the stallion depot at Mazagan. At first I thought of assigning him to Sergeant-Major C—, a good light-weight rider, but was amazed to find that this superb Anglo-Arab was vicious and dangerous. I saw that he might kill his rider by rearing and falling backwards—a trick he used whenever asked to leave the stable or to travel without the company of other horses.

Although too heavy for this young horse, I rode him for an hour one day. I became absolutely convinced that he was neither vicious nor dangerous. He was simply frightened. I assigned him to a tall but light-weight soldier (a Moroccan, as were all the rest). This soldier was the biggest coward at the depot. I instructed him to ride Fabricius while the stallions were being exercised, and little by little to ride him away from them. I cautioned him that he was not to seem to make any demands whatever on the horse. I told him to grab the pommel at the first sign of rebellion, and above all forbade him annoying or nagging the horse. The soldier was not long in getting confidence; the horse likewise, and in a few days they understood each other perfectly. What a treat to see the height from which that same cowardly Larbi ben Mohammed, mounted on Fabricius become now fit for a king, looked down upon the French non-commissioned officers and his Moslem comrades! What a picture Fabricius, with his beautiful head carriage, his "look of eagles," his magnificent sweep of neck, and his tail earned as only the pure bred horse of the East can carry it!

He was superb, and so gentle, that after being classed as a non-breeder he was assigned to Battalion Chief B— a man of great talent in many lines, but not in riding.

CYRANO: A well-shaped gray Barb, 15 hands, belonging to Veterinarian D— who had made the horse so stubborn that he could not be got out of the veterinary infirmary located in the outskirts of Mazagan. One day a young army paymaster undertook to conquer Cyrano, but after several trials he could not force the horse past the Remount depot. Cyrano would back furiously; there was real danger in attempting to force him.

I mounted Cyrano at the same infirmary. He left it quietly, without any hesitation, and never thought of stopping in front of the depot. I rode him for a few miles along the Azemmour road and back to the depot. I had him led to the infirmary by an old experienced soldier, the best man in the company. This soldier was given the task of training the horse. He was to ride with reins on the horse's neck; to ask nothing at all of the horse, which was to be allowed to go as he pleased to the stallion exercise ground. There he was to be ridden at the walk in all directions, but at a distance from the other horses; for the return trip, different roads and trails were to be used. Relying on the soldier's discretion, I afterward ordered him to ride Cyrano for hours at the walk, and later at the trot all about the country, through Arab villages, etc. I especially cautioned him against trying to guide or direct the horse. I told him to mind his own business; to think of anything except the horse; to be only a passenger. Some days later Cyrano was not balky. Six months later I saw the horse at the mobile Remount depot at Casablanca. He was the pride and delight of the noncommissioned officers; they were getting him ready for the coming horse show, and he was jumping well.

The moral of this tale is: instead of trying to apply with much ado the principles of mechanics, encourage the horse to believe that nothing is being required of him; keep him, unwitting, in this frame of mind; let him believe, while obeying you, that he is the master.

On the other hand, if the horse feels that a defense or a hesitation is EXPECTED, one or both are sure to occur. When trying to leave stables with a horse that usually balks upon leaving, if the rider involuntarily closes his legs, or takes hold on the reins, or changes position in the saddle; the horse, warned by the mental attitude of his rider, at once thinks of NOT GOING; he even makes up his mind to kick if his rider attempts to force him. So it is with a timid horse whose rider expects him to shy at a certain object; and with a jigging horse whose rider is busy trying to MAKE the horse walk, instead of paying no attention to him and LETTING him walk of his own accord.

ARNEB: A dappled gray Moroccan, owned for many years by a civil functionary at Settat. The horse was sent to me, the owner said, because he would not change leads at the gallop, and because he had taken to rearing, and had become dangerous. As a matter of fact, the horse did throw the man who was bringing him to me, and ran away. When caught, thanks to a mare that was passing, I rode him and saw that he was an inveterate and exclusive left-galloper. He would get back on his haunches and begin rearing if not allowed to gallop left. I could not make him take the right lead, and at dark I took him to the stable. The owner there explained that in saying the horse would not change leads, he had meant he would not gallop on the right lead.

On the second day I could not get the right lead. Arneb wanted to rear instead of obeying. I quit attempting the right lead and tried the *passage.* Finally, I got him into a passage, and then had no trouble in making him take the right lead.

The third day he would take either lead on a circle.

The fourth day I rode him to Benhammed. It was very hot, and the journey of about twenty-eight miles, up and down hill on a road that was a veritable bed of stones, was far from being play for Arneb.

At Benhammed I told the wagon train sergeant about Arneb. The sergeant was interested and decided to ride with me on my return the next morning. During the ride I invited the sergeant to ride Arneb. After a trial the sergeant said the horse knew nothing—was impossible. I told the sergeant to follow my instructions; to take the snaffle reins and adjust them with his hands at about the pommel of the saddle; to FIX his hands without pulling; to close his legs as if he meant to take the trot. At the second trial the horse went into a *passage.* Many times during the ride the sergeant put him to the passage, always exclaiming, "How extraordinary! How astonishing!"

When the sergeant finally dismounted, he said to me, "Then the half turns, the two tracks, etc.—all that is hokum." I replied, "No," and explained to him that an expert horsemen demanded a supple horse; one capable of a good school exhibition, and that the various school movements were necessary to this end.

On the contrary, a hunter or park horse does not require a course of suppling. The park horse should know how to take and to maintain the gait desired by his rider; how to slow the gallop easily; how to show himself well, and if he is to be exceptionally good, he should *passage,* and change easily at the gallop. For these requirements, he has merely to be taught to go forward at the call of the rider's legs.

On the sixth day I met a retired cavalry soldier at Settat, and asked him to ride Arneb and to notice his utter ignorance of the training exercises prescribed in drill regulations. The soldier complied. I then directed him:

Captain Carr, U.S.A.

1. To set the horse's head to the right, and to use both legs simultaneously for the right gallop; for the left gallop, to set his head to the left, etc.
2. Being at the gallop, to shift the horse's head-set, being careful to maintain his own seat very straight, and to keep both legs equally close to the horse, but passive.
3. To fix both hands on the reins; to avoid pulling; to close both legs equally and simultaneously.

The soldier, who rode without spurs, followed direction and obtained: gallop-departs on each lead; changes of leg in the air, and the *passage.* He was as happy as he was astonished, and asked me as a favor to ride his horse Abderrham, when I had time.

I returned Arneb to his owner, and thereafter every time we met he would say, "You have trained my horse; that, I can understand, but the incredible part is that he works as well for me as he did for you."

A month later I rode Arneb again. He was still the same insensitive horse, with his long, horizontal neck and shaggy

A Triple: precise, accurate, easy. Captain Bradford, U. S. A., up.

overhanging mane. One might have thought he was a wooden horse. Nevertheless, on straight lines and on very small figures of eight he galloped like an old timer of the *menage;* he executed repeated changes of lead at every third or second stride, but never changed until asked. On a figure of eight he passaged with imperturbable calm.

ABDERRHAM: An Algerian Barb stallion, flea bitten gray, fourteen years old, and spavined. He had been condemned as used up, and sold by the constabulary. He was a puller, broke his gaits, and went into a bad sort of pace whenever the reins were touched, or at the approach of a mare. I rode him about 11 o'clock on a very hot morning—the first time he had been out of his stall in several days. Some mares and foals came near us. He jammed his head down, and when I tried to put him into a gallop he went to pieces, but finally took a disordered gallop. The next, day I gave him another lesson, and obtained a horribly rough *passage,* a left gallop, and, with great difficulty, a poor right gallop on a circle.

Two or three days later the soldier rode him, and found him perfect. His *passage* was easy, elastic, brilliant; he galloped, as the soldier said, "like a real general's horse." My greatest difficulty had been to get him to hold the outside lead on a circle. When I had finished, he would take the gallop smoothly, and hold it, or change at the rider's will, on serpentines, figures of eight, etc. He would change leads as often as one wished, every four, three, or two strides. It is said that repeated changes of lead are very tiring and hard on the loins. This old horse would execute many figures of eight, changing leads at every change of direction. He handled himself easily at the *passage,* a gait at which, all of a sudden, he had become brilliant.

His owner, in his own words, was "enchanted, amazed." A few days later he sold the horse at an un-hoped for price to a former officer of the French Remount Service.

DRUZE: A dappled gray stallion, 15 hands, foaled 1916, by Fahed, a pure Arabian, out of Bakta, a mare in the Moroccan Stud Book.

Druze was the last horse I rode in Morocco. He belonged to M. Couderc, the tax assessor at Settat. The retired soldier, the owner of Abderrham, had been entrusted with Druze's training and had taught the horse to stand for mounting, and to go quietly at the walk and trot.

Unfortunately, after the departure of this trainer, Druze was ridden by some ignorant Europeans. When he commenced to show signs of intractability, this small, breedy, sensitive little horse was turned over to a Moroccan "horseman," and soon lost all the sense he had left.

He could not be ridden even at a walk; he would become mad; violently throw his head, and by jamming it down, would almost jerk the rider's arms off. His so-called trainer always returned him to the stable wet with sweat. The horse went off his feed, and it is easy to imagine what he became under such a regime.

One year after the departure of the first trainer, I began to ride the horse. I would have quickly given him up had I not been anxious to be of service to his owner. I did well in persisting, for in two months he had changed completely. He was back on his feed; at his normal weight, full of power, and his gaits were good.

His owner had shown wisdom in telling me that he did not boast of being an expert rider; that all he wanted was a horse that he could ride quietly at the three gaits. Knowing that not the slightest lightness would ever be demanded of Druze, I did no work on his mouth. I rode him in the large four-ring snaffle he had on when brought to me—bitting much too heavy for his small mouth.

Within a few months the horse was going perfectly at the three gaits; he would pass anything; his head-carriage was steady; his neck, horizontal at the walk, was elevated a little at the trot and gallop.

Druze was additional evidence that I am not mistaken in saying that the supplings generally adopted in training horses are superfluous in the making of a pleasant, agreeable riding horse.

Druze would gallop on either lead; maintain very regularly the desired speed—whether rapid or very slow. He would turn short at the true or the counter gallop, or change legs, as the rider desired. On small circles, without apparent movement of rider's aids, and without shifting his haunches the least bit, he would change leads at every fourth, third or second stride—all of this without flexion of the jaw, without any setting of head or neck, which remained in their natural positions. He had never been suppled, he had done no school exercise, and he was ridden in a large snaffle bit, much too heavy for him.

M. Couderc rode Druze in my company. He obtained good gaits while hacking, and then, doing as I said, he started Druze at a gallop at the desired speed and on the desired foot; he effortlessly rode the horse on turns and circles at the true or the counter gallop, and finally had no difficulty in obtaining several changes of lead on a circle by simply displacing his hands.

What conclusions are to be drawn?

CONCLUSIONS

That the easiest way is often the best; the simplest means are generally the most effectual. Horses trained by such means *can be ridden by anyone.*

On the contrary, the application of mathematical principles is difficult. I, for one, would never undertake to train a horse, if obliged to calculate, and then to coordinate the action of my two legs, and two reins with the displacements of my seat, in order to obtain a gait or maneuver of the horse.

In my humble opinion, the pursuit of a learned and abstruse procedure in the ordinary training of a horse is the sole cause for such criticisms as follows: "The school system, the *écuyers,* Saumur, have wrought mortal harm to our cavalry."

These words, written by a great military chieftain who, for a long time, was particularly well-situated to observe and to appraise the *écuyers* and their equestrian principles, means this:

The routine of a rigorous military theory and the faint-heartedness of the training given our horses makes them all too often completely impotent when facing the difficulties and dangerous obstacles habitual with our foreign comrades, notably the Italians.

> "It is no exaggeration to say that cavalry officers capable of training a horse properly are as rare as well-trained horses.
>
> "Upon leaving Saumur, officers possess boldness, leadership, firmness; but the principles of horse-training have little place in the instruction given at this school, and consequently are scarcely included in those qualities which go to make up and complete the cavalry officer."
>
> "How quickly the bold and energetic horses, the very best in our ranks, wear themselves out or become stubborn and balky!
>
> "The poor training of our cavalry horses costs France millions of francs."

Photograph by Fotograms.
Major Doak, U. S. A., on Joffre
Joffre to Major Doak: "You can't help me, don't try. All I ask of you is not to hinder me." The request was obeyed.

The method of training which I have presented quickly gives surprising results, and proves the superiority of a procedure that triumphs, without struggle, without complications in the use of the aids, over all resistances of the horse. In some cases, many of the exercises which I have outlined are superfluous.

The outdoor horse—the horse of service—the hunter, the park horse, etc., should be light, solely because when light he can better coordinate and husband his power and energy; but it is superfluous to put him through a course of suppling exercises, such as work on two tracks, the *rassembler* or the *piaffer*. He merely has to know how to take and to maintain the desired gait; to increase or decrease it quietly and easily; how to jump well, to carry himself elegantly when the occasion demands; and if he is to be a "topper," how to *passage* and to change leads correctly at the gallop.

All these requirements are inborn in the horse; therefore there is nothing to teach him. It is merely a question of having him understand that we want the execution of a movement he [already] knows.

For him to understand the rider's wishes, it suffices to habituate him to move forward at the call of the rider's legs, while remaining light to his hands. Then he will immediately respond to every demand, if he is not cramped or otherwise annoyed.

Really, what must be learned? To take the desired lead at the gallop? That, with a straight horse, is obtained by impulsion acting on the position given by the reins. The change of leg at the gallop? That, with a straight horse, is merely the influence of a change of position on impulsion. The *passage?* That is simply impulsion acting on a fixed hand.

There is nothing else to teach him.

On the other hand, many of the airs of the *haute école* are artificial. To obtain them, it is only logical to profit by the teachings of the great masters. Yet these airs, which so amaze the crowd, are often a mere trifle.

Anything in the way?
Tan Bark over a Difficult 4' 8", Major Chamberlin, U. S. A., up.
Note the straight line from elbow to bit, the ease and alertness of horse and rider. This picture, more accurately than words, describes the *sine qua non* of riding, "Being with the horse."

> *"For the connoisseur, perfection lies in the purity of movement, rather than in the execution of* tours de force, *which convention is pleased to call equestrian difficulties."* (General L'Hotte)

Be that as it may, the key to the mysteries of the *haute école* is LIGHTNESS, obtained without IMPAIRING IMPULSION in the slightest degree. Lightness permits the realization of the *piaffer*, the gallop in place without use of hand or leg-aids. Genius must do the rest, and if seconded by assiduous work, gives *to the natural gaits all of their exquisite beauty.*

Therefore, everywhere—out-of-doors or in the *haute école*—success with horses is to him who applies this maxim of Baucher, whom General L'Hotte described as that inimitable artist who amazed his contemporaries:

> "'Let him think that he is our master, then he is our slave." There dwells an eternal equestrian truth!

> *"The horse is the sole master of his forces; even with all of our vigor, by himself, the rider is powerless to increase the horse's forces. Therefore, it is for the horse to employ his forces in his own way, for himself to determine the manner of that employment so as best to fulfill the demands of his rider. If the rider tries to do it all, the horse may permit him to do so, but the horse merely drifts, and limits his efforts to those which the rider demands. On the contrary, if the horse knows that he must rely on himself, he uses his himself completely, with all of his energy."*

5 May, 1922.

www.ingramcontent.com/pod-product-compliance
Lightning Source LLC
Chambersburg PA
CBHW050556300426
44112CB00013B/1940